IRRIGATION PRACTICES AND SUSTAINABLE AGRICULTURE

ENV BOOKS SERIES

IRRIGATION PRACTICES AND SUSTAINABLE AGRICULTURE

Editors

Dr. Prasann Kumar

Division of Research and Development
Lovely Professional University
Jalandhar - 144 411 (Punjab)
(India)

&

Dr. Pawan Kumar 'Bharti'

Society for Environment, Health Awareness of
Nutrition & Toxicology (SEHAT)
B-225/5D, Top Floor, Subhash Gali, Road No. 7, Block B
Ashok Nagar, Shahdara, Delhi - 110 093
(India)

DPH

DISCOVERY PUBLISHING HOUSE PVT. LTD.
INDIA

Published by:
Namit Wasan

DISCOVERY PUBLISHING HOUSE PVT. LTD.
4383/4B, Ansari Road, Darya Ganj
New Delhi-110 002 (India)
Phone : +91-11-23279245; 23253475; 43596065
E-mail : discoverybooksindia@gmail.com
discoverypublishinghouse@gmail.com
namitwasan9@gmail.com
web : www.discoverypublishinggroup.com

First Edition: **2020**

ISBN: 978-93-88854-31-3

Irrigation Practices and Sustainable Agriculture

Printed at:
Infinity Imaging Systems
Delhi

M.S. Swaminathan Research Foundation

M.S. Swaminathan
Founder Chairman
Ex-Member of Parliament (Rajya Sabha)

Foreword

I am very glad to know that a several books are being edited under the aegis of ENVBOOKS series, Delhi, India on various sub-themes of Agriculture and environment like:

'Cultivation Techniques for Agriculture Crops'

'Air Pollution and Control'

'Seed and Food Storage Technologies'

'Heavy Metals and Impacts on Plants'

'Climate Change and Agriculture Production'

'Scientific Writing and Research Methodology'

'Laboratory Management'

'Statistical Tools in Science'

'Advances in Chemistry and Chemical Sciences'

'Irrigation techniques in Crop management' 'Waste Management Practices'

'Vermitechnology, Farm and Fertilizers'

'Animal Science and Pest Control'

'Recent Research in Biochemistry and Molecular Biology'

'Water Management and Sustainability'

'Soil Quality and Agriculture'

I am very happy to learn that a number of editors and authors from different institutions and university of different nations are involved in editing these books. The books are the compendium of screened-in manuscripts received from different countries like UK, Canada, Egypt, Nigeria, Ghana, Ethiopia, China, South Africa, Japan, Guyana, PNG, Nepal, South America, and various parts of India. I am feeling delighted in writing forward to these books and congratulate to Dr. Pawan Kumar Bharti, Editor-in-Chief and founder of ENVBOOKS series and of course his team for their tenacity and hard work in compiling these valuable compendiums.

I hope these books will be beneficial for academician, researchers, industrialist, policy makers and students as study material and will work as reference for further research work.

M.S. Swaminathan

Preface

Irrigation was used as a means of manipulation of water in the alluvial plains of the Indus valley civilization, the application of it is estimated to have begun around 4500 BC and drastically increased the size and prosperity of their agricultural settlements.

Irrigation systems are also used for cooling livestock, dust suppression, disposal of sewage, and in mining. Irrigation is often studied together with drainage, which is the removal of surface and sub-surface water from a given area. Irrigation has been a central feature of agriculture for over 5,000 years and is the product of many cultures.

Sustainable agriculture is farming in sustainable ways (meeting society's food and textile needs in the present without compromising the ability of future generations to meet their own needs) based on an understanding of ecosystem services, the study of relationships between organisms and their environment. It is a long-term methodological structure that incorporates profit, environmental stewardship, fairness, health, business and familial aspects on a farm setting.

The most important factors for an individual site are climate, soil, nutrients, and water. Of the four, water and soil quality and quantity are most amenable to human intervention through time and labor. When farmers grow and harvest crops, they remove some nutrients from the soil. Without replenishment, land suffers from nutrient depletion and becomes either unusable or suffers from reduced yields. Sustainable agriculture depends on replenishing the soil while minimizing the use or need of non-renewable resources.

The present book updates the subject content on Conservation Technology in Rainfed Production System, Impact of Agricultural Drainage Water on Crops, Waterlogging Stress in Maize, Organic Nutrient-Management Practices in Rice–Tomato–Okra System under Irrigated Conditions, Water Use Efficiency and Stress of Salinity, Sustainable Agriculture for the Sustainable Life on Earth, Agricultural Development, Green Revolution, Hydro Power for Sustainable Development.

Thanks are due to publisher and contributors from various institutions and universities.

The book will be helpful for the researchers, academia working in the field of Conservation Technology in Rainfed System, Impact of Drainage Water on Crops, Waterlogging Stress in Maize, Organic Nutrient-Management Practices, Water Use Efficiency and Stress of Salinity, Sustainable Agriculture, Sustainable Development, Agricultural Development and Green Revolution.

–Editors

(envbooks@gmail.com)

Contents

Introduction

Irrigation is the application of controlled amounts of water to plants at needed intervals. Irrigation helps to grow agricultural crops, maintain landscapes, and revegetate disturbed soils in dry areas and during periods of less than average rainfall. Irrigation also has other uses in crop production, including frost protection, suppressing weed growth in grain fields and preventing soil consolidation. In contrast, agriculture that relies only on direct rainfall is referred to as rain-fed or dry land farming.

Irrigation systems are also used for cooling livestock, dust suppression, disposal of sewage, and in mining. Irrigation is often studied together with drainage, which is the removal of surface and sub-surface water from a given area. Irrigation has been a central feature of agriculture for over 5,000 years and is the product of many cultures. Historically, it was the basis for economies and societies across the globe.

Irrigation was used as a means of manipulation of water in the alluvial plains of the Indus valley civilization, the application of it is estimated to have begun around 4500 BC and drastically increased the size and prosperity of their agricultural settlements. The Indus Valley Civilization developed sophisticated irrigation and water-storage systems, including artificial reservoirs at Girnar dated to 3000 BCE, and an early canal irrigation system from 2600 BCE. Large-scale agriculture was practiced, with an extensive network of canals used for the purpose of irrigation.

Farmers in the Mesopotamian plain used irrigation from at least the third millennium BCE. They developed perennial irrigation, regularly watering crops throughout the growing season by coaxing water through a matrix of small channels formed in the field. Ancient Egyptians practiced basin irrigation using the flooding of the Nile to inundate land plots which had been surrounded by dykes. The flood water remained until the fertile sediment had settled before the engineers returned the surplus to the watercourse. There is evidence of the ancient Egyptian pharaoh Amenemhet III in the twelfth dynasty (about 1800 BCE) using the natural lake of the Faiyum Oasis as a reservoir to store surpluses of water for use during dry seasons. The lake swelled annually from the flooding of the Nile.

Types of Irrigation

There are several methods of irrigation. They vary in how the water is supplied to the plants. The goal is to apply the water to the plants as uniformly as possible, so that each plant has the amount of water it needs, neither too much nor too little.

Surface Irrigation

Surface irrigation is the oldest form of irrigation and has been in use for thousands of years. In surface (flood, or level basin) irrigation systems, water moves across the surface of an agricultural lands, in order to wet it and infiltrate into the soil. Surface irrigation can be subdivided into furrow, border strip or basin irrigation. It is often called flood irrigation when the irrigation results in flooding or near flooding of the cultivated land. Historically, this has been the most common method of irrigating agricultural land and is still used in most parts of the world.

Where water levels from the irrigation source permit, the levels are controlled by dikes, usually plugged by soil. This is often seen in terraced rice fields (rice paddies), where the method is used to flood or control the level of water in each distinct field. In some cases, the water is pumped, or lifted by human or animal power to the level of the land. The water application efficiency of surface irrigation is typically lower than other forms of irrigation.

Surface irrigation is even used to water landscapes in certain areas, for example, in and around Phoenix, Arizona. The irrigated area is surrounded by a berm and the water is delivered according to a schedule set by a local irrigation district.

Micro-irrigation

Micro-irrigation, sometimes called localized irrigation, low volume irrigation, or trickle irrigation is a system where water is distributed under low pressure through a piped network, in a pre-determined pattern, and applied as a small discharge to each plant or adjacent to it. Traditional drip irrigation using individual emitters, subsurface drip irrigation (SDI), micro-spray or micro-sprinkler irrigation, and mini-bubbler irrigation all belong to this category of irrigation methods.

Drip Irrigation

Drip (or micro) irrigation, also known as trickle irrigation, functions as its name suggests. In this system water falls drop by drop just at the position of roots. Water is delivered at or near the root zone of plants, drop by drop. This method can be the most water-efficient method of irrigation, if managed properly, evaporation and runoff are minimized. The field water efficiency of drip irrigation is typically in the range of 80 to 90 percent when managed correctly.

In modern agriculture, drip irrigation is often combined with plastic mulch, further reducing evaporation, and is also the means of delivery of fertilizer. The process is known as fertigation.

Deep percolation, where water moves below the root zone, can occur if a drip system is operated for too long or if the delivery rate is too high. Drip irrigation methods range from very high-tech and computerized to low-tech and labor-intensive. Lower water pressures are usually needed than for most other types of systems, with the exception of low energy center pivot systems and surface irrigation systems, and the system can be designed for uniformity throughout a field or for precise water delivery to individual plants in a landscape containing a mix of plant species. Although it is difficult to regulate pressure on steep slopes, pressure compensating emitters are available, so the field does not have to be level. High-tech solutions involve precisely calibrated emitters located along lines of tubing that extend from a computerized set of valves.

Sprinkler Irrigation

In sprinkler or overhead irrigation, water is piped to one or more central locations within the field and distributed by overhead high-pressure sprinklers or guns. A system using sprinklers, sprays, or guns mounted overhead on permanently installed risers is often referred to as a solid-set irrigation system. Higher pressure sprinklers that rotate are called rotors and are driven by a ball drive, gear drive, or impact mechanism. Rotors can be designed to rotate in a full or partial circle. Guns are similar to rotors, except that they generally operate at very high pressures of 275 to 900 kPa (40 to 130 psi) and flows of 3 to 76 L/s (50 to 1200 US gal/min), usually with nozzle diameters in the range of 10 to 50 mm (0.5 to 1.9 in). Guns are used not only for irrigation, but also for industrial applications such as dust suppression and logging.

Sprinklers can also be mounted on moving platforms connected to the water source by a hose. Automatically moving wheeled systems known as traveling sprinklers may irrigate areas such as small farms, sports fields, parks, pastures, and cemeteries unattended. Most of these use a length of polyethylene tubing wound on a steel drum. As the tubing is wound on the drum powered by the irrigation water or a small gas engine, the sprinkler is pulled across the field. When the sprinkler arrives back at the reel the system shuts off. This type of system is known to most people as a "waterreel" traveling irrigation sprinkler and they are used extensively for dust suppression, irrigation, and land application of waste water.

Other travelers use a flat rubber hose that is dragged along behind while the sprinkler platform is pulled by a cable.

Sustainable Agriculture

Sustainable agriculture is farming in sustainable ways (meeting society's food and textile needs in the present without compromising the ability of future generations to meet their own needs) based on an understanding of ecosystem services, the study of relationships between organisms and their environment. It is a long-term methodological structure that incorporates profit, environmental stewardship, fairness, health, business and familial aspects on a farm setting. It is defined by 3 integral aspects which are: economic profit, environmental stewardship and social responsibility. Sustainability focuses on the business process and practice of a farm in general, rather than a specific agricultural product. The integrated economic, environmental, and social principles are incorporated into a "triple bottom line" (TBL); when the general impacts of the farm are assessed. Unlike a traditional approach where the profit-margin is the single major factor; Agriculture sustainability is also involved with the social and environmental factors.

Sustainable agriculture can be understood as an ecosystem approach to agriculture. Practices that can cause long-term damage to soil include excessive tilling of the soil (leading to erosion) and irrigation without adequate drainage (leading to salinization). Long-term experiments have provided some of the best data on how various practices affect soil properties essential to sustainability. In the United States a federal agency, USDA-Natural Resources Conservation Service, specializes in providing technical and financial assistance for those interested in pursuing natural resource conservation and production agriculture as compatible goals.

The most important factors for an individual site are climate, soil, nutrients, and water. Of the four, water and soil quality and quantity are most amenable to human intervention through time and labor. When farmers grow and harvest crops, they remove some nutrients from the soil. Without replenishment, land suffers from nutrient depletion and becomes either unusable or suffers from reduced yields. Sustainable agriculture depends on replenishing the soil while minimizing the use or need of non-renewable resources, such as natural gas (used in converting atmospheric nitrogen into synthetic fertilizer), or mineral ores (e.g., phosphate). Possible sources of nitrogen that would, in principle, be available indefinitely, include:

- recycling crop waste and livestock or treated human manure
- growing legume crops and forages such as peanuts or alfalfa that form symbioses with nitrogen-fixing bacteria called rhizobia
- industrial production of nitrogen by the Haber process uses hydrogen, which is currently derived from natural gas (but this hydrogen could instead be made by electrolysis of water using renewable electricity, or
- genetically engineering (non-legume) crops to form nitrogen-fixing symbioses or fix nitrogen without microbial symbionts.

The last option was proposed in the 1970s, but is only gradually becoming feasible. Sustainable options for replacing other nutrient inputs such as phosphorus and potassium are more limited.

More realistic, and often overlooked, options include long-term crop rotations, returning to natural cycles that annually flood cultivated lands (returning lost nutrients indefinitely) such as the flooding of the Nile, the long-term use of biochar, and use of crop and livestock landraces that are adapted to less than ideal conditions such as pests, drought, or lack of nutrients. Crops that require high levels of soil nutrients can be cultivated in a more sustainable manner with appropriate fertilizer management practices.

Socioeconomic aspects of sustainability are also partly understood. Regarding less concentrated farming, the best known analysis is Netting's study on smallholder systems through history.

Given the finite supply of natural resources at any specific cost and location, agriculture that is inefficient or damaging to needed resources may eventually exhaust the available resources or the ability to afford and acquire them. It may also generate negative externality, such as pollution as well as financial and production costs. There are several studies incorporating these negative externalities in an economic analysis concerning ecosystem services, biodiversity, land degradation and sustainable land management. These include The Economics of Ecosystems and Biodiversity study led by Pavan Sukhdev and the Economics of Land Degradation Initiative which seeks to establish an economic cost benefit analysis on the practice of sustainable land management and sustainable agriculture.

The way that crops are sold must be accounted for in the sustainability equation. Food sold locally does not require additional energy for transportation (including consumers). Food sold at a remote location, whether at a farmers' market or the supermarket, incurs a different set of energy cost for materials, labour, and transport.

Pursuing sustainable agriculture results in many localized benefits. Having the opportunities to sell products directly to consumers, rather than at wholesale or commodity prices, allows farmers to bring in optimal profit.

Triple bottom line frameworks (including social and environmental aspects alongside the financial) show that a sustainable company can be technologically and economically feasible. For this to happen, growth in material consumption and population need to be slowed down and there has to be a drastic increase in the efficiency of material and energy use. To make that transition, long- and short-term goals will need to be balanced enhancing equity and quality of life.

References

https://en.wikipedia.org/wiki/Irrigation

https://www.civilserviceindia.com/subject/General-Studies/notes/different-types-of-irrigation-and-irrigation-systems-storage.html

https://en.wikipedia.org/wiki/Sustainable_agriculture

https://asi.ucdavis.edu/programs/ucsarep/about/what-is-sustainable-agriculture

Section I: Irrigation Practices

Pages: 3-16

Irrigation Practices and Sustainable Agriculture
Edited by: **Dr. Prasann Kumar and Dr. Pawan Kumar 'Bharti'**
ISBN: 978-93-88854-31-3
Edition: **2020**
Published by: **Discovery Publishing House Pvt. Ltd., New Delhi (India)**

1 Conservation Technology in Rainfed Production System

Prasann Kumar[1, 2*] and Johnson Yumnam[1]

GRAPHICAL ABSTRACT

Keywords: Agriculture, Conservation, Production, Rainfed, Technology

INTRODUCTION

Convergence of Opinions

- Demand for food - increasing
- Harvested area - possibly shrinking

[1] Department of Agronomy, School of Agriculture, Lovely Professional University, Jalandhar - 144 411 (Punjab) (India)

[2] Divison of Research and Development, Lovely Professional University, Jalandhar - 144 411 (Punjab) (India)

- Traditional sources of productivity growth – are they *exhausted?*
- More competitionfor water
- Costs for fuel and inputs rising
- More severe weatheras a result of GHG emissions and global climate change
- In addition, there is resource and environmental degradation?

Challenges for Agriculture

- To increase food production more efficiently and sustainably to meet food security needs while minimizing the effects on the environment and improving the livelihoods of those involved in agriculture
- This will require more efficient use of resources and maintaining a healthy soil.

Sustainability Issues

- Declining and deterioration of natural resources (NRs)
- Shrinking farm profitability
- Declining factor productivity
- Nutrient mining and multiple nutrient deficiencies
- Over exploitation of ground water resources
- Soil degradation due to intensive wet tillage practices
- Decrease in soil organic carbon
- Pest buildup due to monotonous cropping systems
- Nutritional insecurity
- Decreasing biodiversity
- Environmental problems

Rainfed Production System

- In India, out of 142.2 m ha net cultivated area, about 87 m ha is unirrigated.
- Rainfed areas produces about 44% of total food requirement.
- Most of the essential commodities such as coarse cereals (90%), pulses (87%) and oil seeds (74%) are produced from the rainfed agriculture.
- In view of the stagnating productivity levels of irrigated agriculture, the contribution from the rainfed agriculture should increase to meet the requirement of the growing population.
- The rainfed production systems are quite heterogeneous and diverse in terms of land and water management and cropping systems.
- Sealing, crusting, sub-surface hard pans and cracking are the key constraints which cause high erosion and impede infiltration of rainfall.
- The choice and type of tillage largely depend on the soil type and rainfall.

- Leaving crop residue on the surface is another important component of CA, but in rainfed areas due to its competing uses as fodder, little or no residues are available for surface application.
- The key principles of rainfed agriculture rely on soil and water conservation, both essential components of the CA.
- Tillage in rainfed areas is mostly carried out for seed bed preparation and interculture operations for weed control and does not use heavy equipment.
- Though conserving both soil and water are equally important; in low to medium rainfall regions, more priority is given for conservation of rainfall by facilitating better infiltration and reduced runoff.
- The deep tillage once in three years is suggested to promote greater infiltration of rainwater and control weeds.

Conservation Agriculture

- Minimal soil disturbance
- Residue retention
- Sensible crop rotation/innovative cropping system/farming system
- Conservation agriculture (CA) is a concept for resource-saving agricultural crop production that strives to achieve acceptable profits together with high and sustained production levels while concurrently conserving the environ-ment (FAO 2007).
- CA is based on enhancing natural biological processes above and below the ground. Interventions such as mechanical soil tillage are reduced to an absolute minimum, and use of external inputs such as agrochemicals and nutrients of mineral or organic origin are applied at an optimum level and in a way and quantity that does not interfere with, or disrupt, the biological processes.

CA is characterized by four principles:

- Minimum mechanical soil disturbance for erosion control.
- Maintenance of permanent organic soil cover.
- Diversified crop rotations for pest and disease control, conserving bio-diversity.
- Controlling in field traffic for reducing the compaction.

However, in practice, zero tillage and residue retention have emerged as the two cardinal principles of CA.

Conservation Agriculture: At a Glance

- CA is practiced on over 96 m ha area world wide, most of it is in USA, Brazil, Argentina, Canada and Australia.

- Zero till technology has been introduced into India and neighboring countries by Rice-Wheat Consortium and several institutions of the national agricultural research system and it is currently adopted by farmers in over 2 million ha largely in the Indo-Gangetic plains.
- World-wide, CA or no-till farming has spread mostly in the rainfed agriculture. However in India its success is more in irrigated belt of the Indo-Gangetic plains.
- Considering the severe problems of land degradation due to runoff induced soil erosion, rainfed areas particularly in arid and semi-arid regions require the practice of CA more than the irrigated areas in order to ensure a sustainable production.

Conservation Agriculture (CA) Involves

- Dramatic Reduction in tillage
  - Goal – Zero-till or controlled-till seeding systems
- Retention of adequate levels of crop residues on the soil surface
  - Ultimate Goal – Retain sufficient residue on the soil surface to protect the soil from erosion and to enhance long term, sustainable production
- Use of proper and profitable crop rotations
  - Ultimate Goal – Employ economically viable, diversified crop rotations
- Immediate potential economic benefits for farmers

Fig. 1.1: Conservation agriculture
Source: Based on review of literature

Fig. 1.2: Planting zero till
Source: Based on review of literature

Fig. 1.3: Tillage without adequate crop residue
Source: Based on review of literature

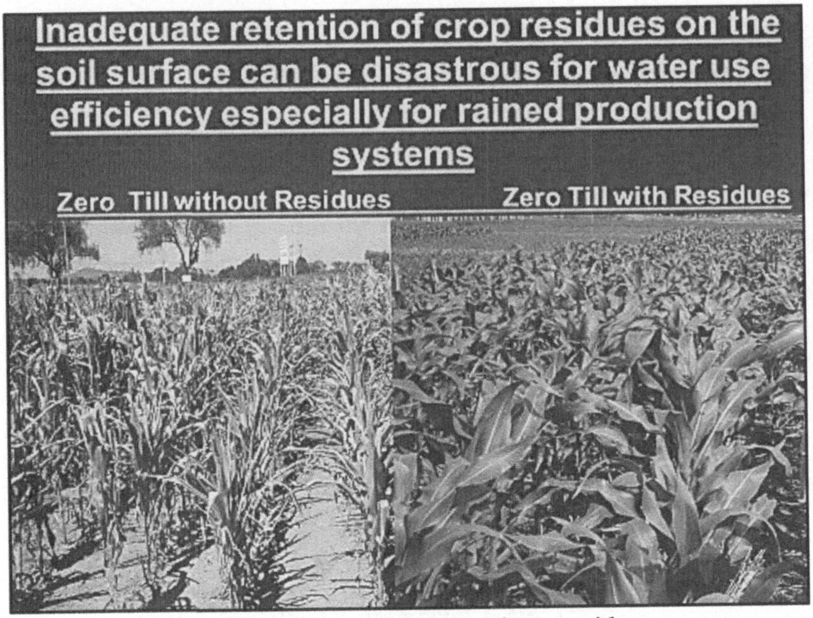

Fig. 1.4: Inadequate retention of crop residue
Source: Based on review of literature

Fig. 1.5: CA is enhanced by diversified economical crop rotations
Source: Based on review of literature

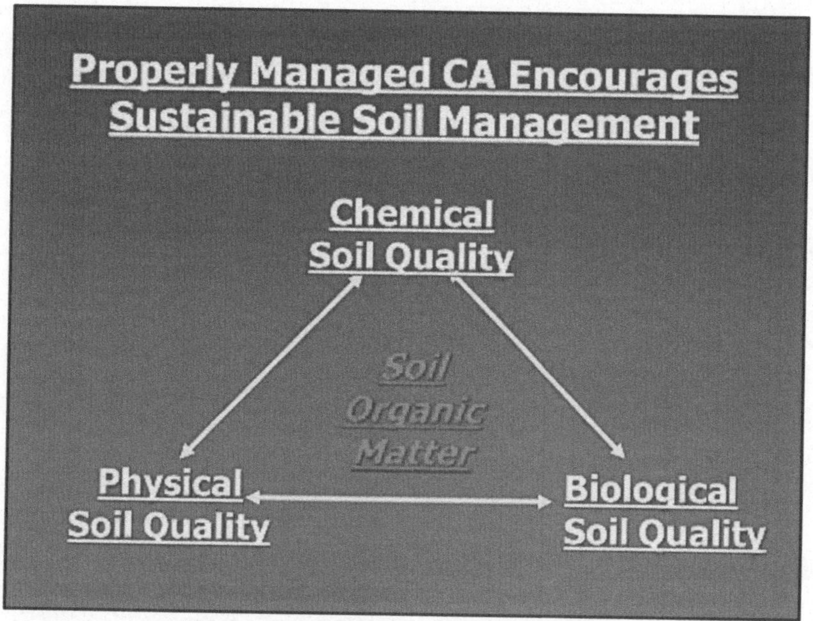

Fig. 1.6: Properly managed CA Encourages
Source: Based on review of literature

CONSERVATION AGRICULTURE (CA) AND RESOURCE CONSERVING TECHNOLOGIES (RCTS)

How are They Related?

- Any new technology delivered to farmers that produces the same or more with less input is an RCT
- Examples of RCTs in general
  - New, higher yielding varieties with good quality and resistances/tolerances to diseases and insects
  - A new pest control practice that controls weeds or insects or diseases more efficiently and/or more cheaply
  - A new fertilizer management practice that provides more yield for less fertilizer
  - A more efficient irrigation system that saves irrigation water but maintains or increases crop yields

Examples of Conservation Agriculture-Based RCTs

- A new planter that allows seeding with reduced or zero tillage
- Development of the technologies to direct seed rice without puddling
- Development of crop varieties that are suitable for zero till seeding

- Development of the management practices needed for farmers to diversify the crop rotations based on zero till planting systems
- Determine the amount of crop residues that should be retained on reduced/zero till fields to improve soil quality and health

CA based RCTs Options for System Sustainability

- Zero tillage
- Paired row
- Control traffic
- Direct seeding
- Unpuddled transplanting
- Reduced tillage
- Bed planting
- Surface seeding

Fig. 1.7: Advantage of Zero Tillage
Source: Based on review of literature

Fig. 1.8: Bed planting
Source: Based on review of literature

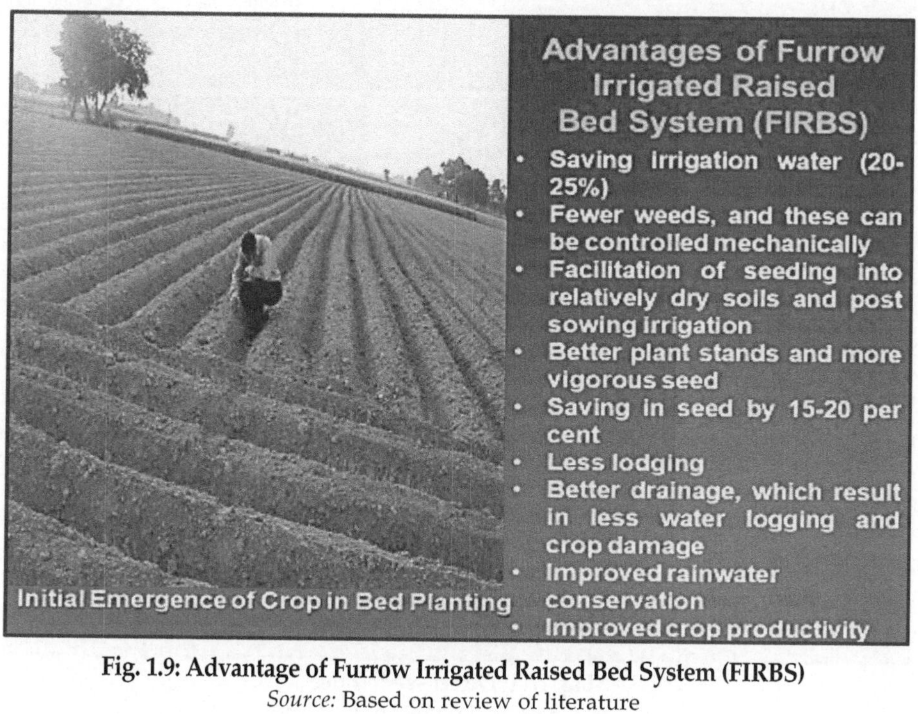

Fig. 1.9: Advantage of Furrow Irrigated Raised Bed System (FIRBS)
Source: Based on review of literature

Fig. 1.10: Direct seeded rice

Source: Based on review of literature

Fig. 1.11: Direct seeded rice

Source: Based on review of literature

Fig. 1.12: Zero tillage drill seeding

Source: Based on review of literature

Benefits of CA based RCTs

- Higher productivity gain
- Good soil health
- Greater reduction in cost of cultivation
- Permanent soil cover
- Minimum soil disturbance
- Minimize seasonal weed infestation

Farming system approach involves integration of:

- Crop
- Livestock
- Trees/forest
- Aquaculture/bee keeping etc.
  - In accordance with physio- graphic/socio-economic suitability and need of the farming community
  - Through effective recycling and/optimal utilization of resources to minimize risk and increase productivity & profitability

Why FSD is needed?

- To develop farm –household systems and rural communities on a sustainable basis
- To improve farm productivity

- To raise farm and family income
- To increase welfare of farm families and satisfy basic needs

Farm–household System

- For FSD, the farm–household is the basic unit for analysis and development because it is the decision making unit which ultimately controls the transfor-mation of inputs into basic agricultural output.
- The farm-household system consists three basic systems which are closely interlinked and interactive.

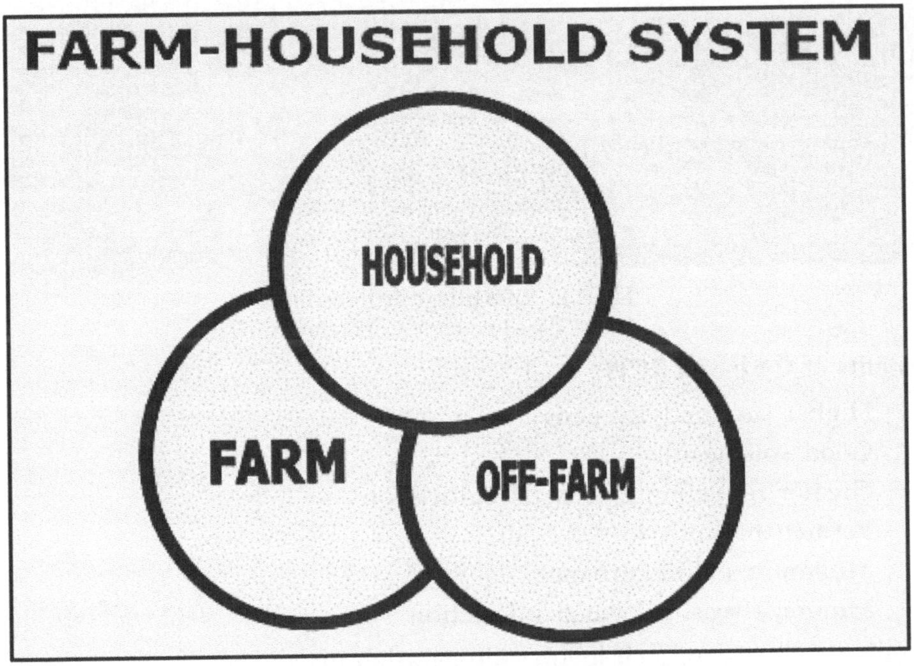

Fig. 1.13: Farm household system

Source: Based on review of literature

Farm–household Systems

- The household is the decision making unit. It establishes goals for the system. It also control the system by providing labour, demanding food and cash in fulfillment of set objectives.
- The farm and its crops and livestock activities provide employment, food and cash for the farm family.
- Off-farm component which competes with farm activities for labour, provides employment and income generating activities. It becomes increasingly more important to supplement the wellbeing of farm families

Objectives of Farm-household System

- Provision of basic needs
- Satisfaction of social obligations
- Security
- Improved standard of living
- Sustaining the ecosystem for future generations

Farm Household Systems and their Surrounding Environment

Farm-household system do not operate in a vacuum. They are part of and influenced by, other systems, conditions and environments which determine to a large extent both constraints and development potentials of the farm household system.

Physical Environment: Climate, soils, topography, water, vegetation, infrastructure.

Socio-cultural Environment: Community, Culture, Tradition

Policy/Institutional Environment: Policy decisions, political framework, legal framework, agricultural research and extension, agricultural support services- marketing, credit, input supply.

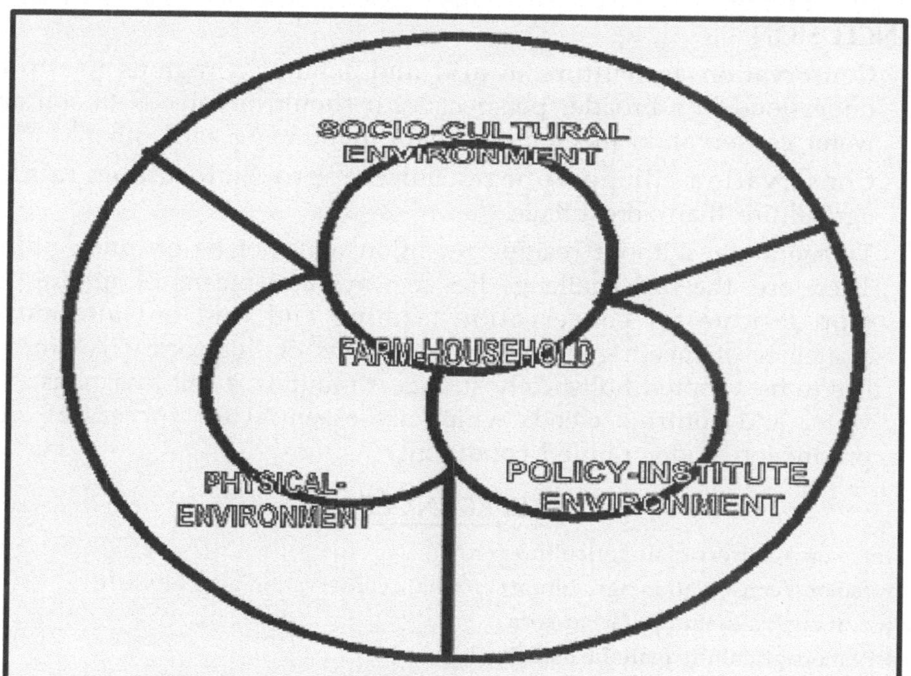

Fig. 1.14: Cross talk among the components
Source: Based on review of literature

Components of FSD

Farming System Analysis (FSA)

- Identifying the connections and interactions between the components of farm household systems, and policy/institutional environ-ments and how they affect the decision making process of farm house level
- Diagnose constraints to increased farm production and productivity
- Identify and assess potential improvement and orient research, extension and supply services or policy makers according to result of FSA
- Farming system planning, monitoring and evaluation
- Testing, monitoring and evaluating improve-ments on-farms
- Planning appropriate improvement in farm-household system
- Disseminating successful practices through extension
- Planning adjustment in support services, research and extension strategies and policy programmes
- Monitoring and evaluating rate of adoption of proposed improvement by the farming community, which is the ultimate success criterion for the approach

CONCLUSION

- Conservation agriculture in arid and semi-arid regions has to be understood in a broader perspective. It should involve both soil and water conservation methods mutually reinforcing each other.
- Conservation tillage appears more appropriate under rainfed agriculture than zero tillage.
- Tillage alone without residue retention may not be of much utility. Therefore, the real challenge lies in ways and means of sparing the crop residue for conservation farming and find out alternative strategies of meeting fodder requirements of livestock. CA practice has to be adopted holistically so that it minimizes soil loss, conserves water and controls weeds which are essential for success of crop production under rainfed conditions.

REFERENCES

www.fao.org/conservation-agriculture/en/

www.fao.org/conservation-agriculture/.../what...conservation-agriculture/e

www.ecaf.org/ca-in-europe/what-is-ca

conservationagriculture.mannlib.cornell.edu/

https://en.wikipedia.org/wiki/Conservation_agriculture

https://www.sciencedirect.com/science/article/pii/S2095633915300538

https://www.sciencedirect.com/topics/agricultural.../conservation-agriculture

https://csa.guide/csa/conservation-agriculture-ca

Pages: 17-36

Irrigation Practices and Sustainable Agriculture
Edited by: **Dr. Prasann Kumar and Dr. Pawan Kumar 'Bharti'**
ISBN: 978-93-88854-31-3
Edition: **2020**
Published by: **Discovery Publishing House Pvt. Ltd., New Delhi (India)**

2 Impact of Agricultural Drainage Water on Crops under Sequential Biological Concentration System

Parameswari, E.*, V. Davamani
S. Paul Sebastian, V. Manivannan[1] and P. Kalaiselvi

INTRODUCTION

Intensive irrigation practices developed during this century have dramatically increased the agricultural productivity. However, these practices have also resulted in increased drainage water production and chemical contamination of groundwater. It is generally acknowledged that long-term agricultural production in irrigated areas is dependent on an adequate drainage outflow system, and a variety of management strategies are currently being considered to reduce the volume of drainage ultimately require disposal or treatment.

Drainage from irrigated land is an inevitable phenomenon, which carries a salt load that was always higher and sometimes substantially higher than irrigation water. Before 1970's, the concern on the part of the scientists was limited to salinity effects on crop productivity and its control within the root zone by leaching and drainage water disposal. During the last two decades, concerns have arisen regarding off-site impacts of irrigation and drainage. Without a viable means of use or disposal, the saline-sodic drainage waters are turning out to be an environmental burden.

A range of methods are available to manage salinity and to rehabilitate saline soils in irrigated regions of which drainage is the most commonly applied phenomena. However, drainage schemes generate large volumes of saline water that must be appropriately managed to prevent production losses and harmful off-site environmental impacts. Community concern over the health of riverine ecosystem are putting pressure on the irrigation industry to minimise saline drainage water entering natural watercourses.

Department of Environmental Sciences, Tamil Nadu Agricultural University, Coimbatore (India)
[1] Department of Agronomy, Tamil Nadu Agricultural University, Coimbatore (India)

Consequently, there is limited capacity to export saline drainage water from inland irrigation regions. This situation necessitates containment and local management of saline drainage water within the irrigated regions. However, studies conducted on the re-use of such water for irrigation have shown promise for crop production systems and soil management. To improve the drainage water management strategy, we have tried the sequential biological concentration system. Hence, in this chapter, the literature on various aspects related to the present study is reviewed under the following headings:

1. Characteristics of agricultural drainage water
2. Reuse of agricultural drainage water for irrigation
3. Sequential Biological Concentration (SBC) system
4. Impact of saline drainage water irrigation on soil and crops
5. Impact of application of amendments on soil and crops
6. Impact of saline water irrigation with amendments on soil and crops
7. Protective mechanism of plants under salinity
8. Effect of drainage water irrigation on groundwater quality
9. Role of halophilic bacteria on crops under salinity

1. Characteristics of agricultural drainage water

The quality of drainage discharge depends on the nature and amount of salts present in the soil profile and the salinity of groundwater. The salt content in the drainage water is variable according to the initial salinity conditions of soil and groundwater and gradually improves with time (Sharma, 2007). The range of EC of drainage water in some drainage projects in India are reported in table 2.1.

Table 2.1: Drainage effluent quality at different locations in India

Station	EC (dS m^{-1})	Station	EC (dS m^{-1})
Karnal (Haryana)	0.5-0.8	Loonkaransar (Rajasthan)	3.5-6.5
Hisar (Haryana)	4.0-8.0	Segwa (Gujarat)	2.0-5.7
Gohana (Haryana)	3.2-5.8	Upper Krishna (Karnatka)	0.8-1.5
Sampla (Haryana)	8.0-27.0	Konanki (Andhara Pradesh)	1.3-2.4
Mundlana (Haryana)	4.1-6.4	Lakhuwali (Rajasthan)	4.5-7.4
Chambal (Rajasthan)	2.0-5.0	Pollachi and Udumalpet (TN)	3.0-3.5

(Sharma, 2007)

Agricultural drainage water is complicated by the presence of soluble organic and inorganic pollutants in addition to hazardous chemicals. Large scale desalination systems for agricultural drainage water require the development of affordable pretreatment for removal of soluble organic matters.The drainage water is not only saline, but may also contain potentially toxic trace elements such as selenium and molybdenum. Ion composition in the saline drainage effluents are predominating in that order of Na^+, SO_4^{2-}, Cl, Mg^{2+} and Ca^{2+}.

The drainage water have only traces of Fe, Mn, Zn, B, absence of P, NH_4^+ and NO_3- N indicated little danger of groundwater pollution as a result of NO_3 and P leaching. The concentration of salts, nutrients and other crop related chemicals in drainage discharge vary with time and discharge rate. The use of fertilizers and pesticides in intensive agricultural production has sometime leads to the damage to downstream ecosystems.

Banuelos and Lin (2006) reported that the drainage water from irrigated areas frequently contains trace elements and salts, in addition to agricultural chemicals. The impacts of salts on downstream users need to be evaluated. Some soils are abundant in trace elements, and these could leach to the drainage system. Small amounts of trace elements such as, Cd, Hg, Pb, B, Cr and Se are harmful to aquatic species because of biological magnification.

2. Reuse of agricultural drainage water for irrigation

Drainage from irrigated land is necessary for sustainable irrigation. Drainage water carries a salt load that is always higher, sometimes substantially higher, than that of the irrigation water. The disposal of the drainage water from irrigation areas needs careful consideration, so that water supplies of downstream are not polluted. Drainage disposal to fresh water bodies is likely to become less acceptable over time hence strategies will have to be considered to manage saline drainage effluent flows from irrigated areas where the salt loads are generated.

In order to make the drainage water re-use strategy successful and environmentally acceptable, there is a need to take into consideration of several management aspects. For instance, an extra quantity of water from irrigation or resulting from a predictable rainfall in excess of that needed for evapotranspiration must be applied as a long-term strategy and done in a manner that does not adversely affect the growing crops. This will prevent excessive accumulation of salts in the root zone. The extra quantity of irrigation water, referred to as leaching requirement, must be able to pass through the root zone. Adequate drainage is an essential criteria for obtaining a desired leaching requirement to maintain soil salinity at levels suitable for crop growth. It also keeps the water table sufficiently deep to permit adequate root development, prevents the net upward flow of salt-laden groundwater into root zone and permits the movement and operations of farm implements in the fields.

The key to use saline-sodic drainagewaters for irrigation would be to grow appropriate salt and Na^+ resistant crops and to maintain soil permeability in order to control soil salinity and sodicity through leaching. The aim behind the successful use of such waters for irrigation would be: (1) to obtain adequate stand and yield of appropriate salt-resistant crops, (2) to control salinity, sodicity and water logging problems in the soil, (3) to maintain soil hydraulic properties and (4) to protect water quality for long-term sustainable agriculture.

Drainage systems can effectively lower water tables and facilitate salt leaching, their use is limited by difficulties with disposal of the drainage water collected. Evaporation ponds are an economical way to store and reduce drainage water, but high levels of selenium (Se) present in drainage water caused deaths and deformities in migratory waterfowl, thereby limiting this option. Among the remaining options proposed for drainage management, reuse for the irrigation of salt-tolerant forages and biodiesel crops such as canola, has emerged as a viable strategy to reduce both the area affected by shallow water tables and the volume of drainage effluent requiring disposal. The feasibility of using drainage water as a resource to produce marketable crops and at the same time, minimize the environmental impacts, has been demonstrated.

Crops differ considerably in their ability to tolerate salinity/sodicity. These intergenic differences can be exploited for selecting the crops that produce satisfactory yield under given levels of root zone salinity and sodicity. Sharma and Rao (1998) found that saline drainage effluent could be used in different modes without appreciable yield reduction in wheat crop. Oilseed crops requiring less water can tolerate higher levels of irrigation water salinity whereas most of the pulses and vegetables are sensitive to salts. The general recommendations for successful use of saline drainage water are, crops that are semi-tolerant to tolerant (mustard, wheat, cotton) as well as those with low water requirement should be grown whereas crops like rice, sugarcane and forages, those require liberal water use, should be avoided.

A number of tree plantations have been used to reclaim sodic soils or to reuse drainage waters as an irrigation source. These include: *Leucaena leucocephala, Prosopis juliflora, Terminalia arjuna, Prosopis cineraria, Dalbergia sissoo* and *Acacia nilotica.*

The provision of subsurface drainage allows the use of saline drainage water through surface applications. Yield reductions were much smaller in fields having a sub-surface drainage system than in fields with a deep water table and the differences were larger at applied water salinities of more than 10 dS m^{-1}. Sub-surface drainage helped in maintaining a more favorable moisture regime in the root zone, which lead to higher productivity (Sharma and Minhas, 2005).

Research has shown that salt tolerant forages can grow well in drainage water reuse systems and supports cattle production. Increased forage production would also meet the needs of the local dairy industry which has expanded rapidly in recent years. However, candidate forages need to be not only salt and boron tolerant, but they must possess sufficient nutritive value as animal feeds.The selection of suitable cultivars is one of the key needs to maintain sustainable forage production systems using saline-sodic waters.

The drainage water reuse was possible during the *rabi* season, consequent to reduction in soil salinity, there was steady increase in the area under cropping as well as yields of *kharif* (sorghum and pearl millet) and *rabi* (berseem and barley, oat) crops.

3. Serial or Sequential Biological Concentration System (SBC)

Serial or Sequential Biological Concentration (SBC) system is a relatively new option for the management of saline drainage water, combining both irrigation reuse and disposal to an evaporation basin. The SBC concept was initially proposed to minimise the size of evaporation basins needed for the disposal of drainage water with high selenium contents in the San Joaquin valley, California. SBC involves the process of irrigating crops in series of increasing crop salt tolerance. Drainage water collected from beneath one crop is used to irrigate the next more salt tolerant crop in the series, with the final highly saline drainage pumped into a small evaporation basin. This concentration process aims to significantly reduce the volume of drainage water and therefore the size of the evaporation basin needed for final disposal. The number of stages used in the design of SBC systems would vary according to the soil and irrigation water salinity, as well as the salt tolerance of the plants used in the system (Figure 2.1).

In California, the sequential reuse experiments have involved the use of trees, shrubs and grasses. Tanji and Karajeh (1993) used a tree–shrub combination by growing *Eucalyptus camaldulensis* with subsurface drain water collected from nearby crop lands (EC 10 dS m^{-1}, SAR 11) while effluents from *Eucalyptus* and the perimeter interceptor drain (EC 32 dS m^{-1}, SAR 69) were used to irrigate *Atriplex* species. The tree plantation were successful in lowering the water table from 0.6 m to 2.3 m while consumptively using the saline-sodic water. But after 5 years of drain water reuse, a substantial buildup of salinity, sodicity and boron occurred throughout the soil profile to the extent that the trees were unable to fully extract the available soil water.

Significant reductions was noticed in growth rate and water use of *Eucalyptus* when irrigated with saline-sodic waters (EC 8-10 dS m^{-1}, SAR 25-30) resulting in average root zone salinities (EC) of 20-22 dS m^{-1}. Two species of *Eucalyptus* (*Eucalyptus occidentalis* and *Eucalyptus sargentii*) were reported to be tolerant to both waterlogging and salinity.

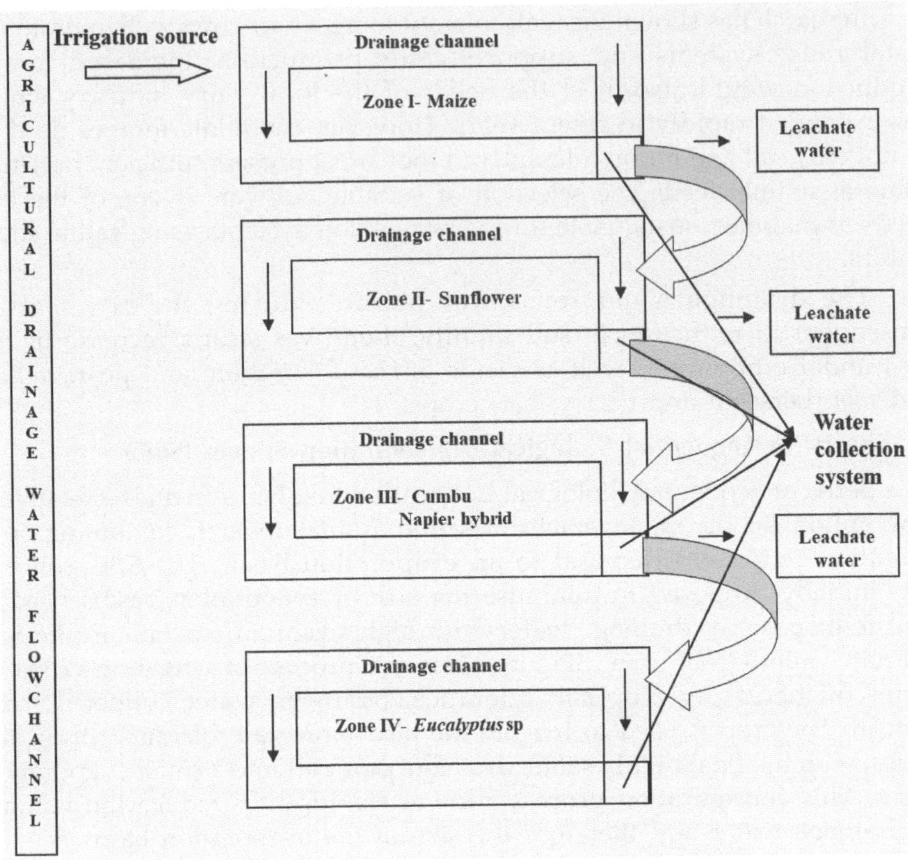

Fig. 2.1: Conceptual diagram of sequential concentration system

Production system based on salt-tolerant forage crops and grasses using saline irrigation water may be sustainable. It has been demonstrated through preliminary experiments that bermuda grass (*Cynodon dactylon*) can be grown with saline-sodic waters having EC approximately 17 dS m^{-1} and SAR exceeding 25. Oster and Birkle (2001) have provided the information regarding growth habit, salt tolerance characteristics, average root zone salinity at 70 per cent yield and leaching requirement of several forages and *Eucalyptus camaldulensis* (clone 4544) when irrigated with a water having salinity of 10 dS m^{-1} and SAR of 15.

The choice of a certain reuse option under SBC system largely depends on drainage water (quantity, quality and time of availability), crop tolerance to salinity and availability of fresh water resources. Reuse of drainage water is challenging from an irrigation management perspective, where the water is both saline (EC 4 dS m^{-1}) and sodic (SAR > 15).

The cyclic strategy of the drainage water re-use involves irrigation of salt-sensitive crops with good-quality water followed by irrigation of salt-resistant crops with saline water. Usually, the saline water is used after the seedling establishment of salt-resistant crops.After the harvest of salt-resistant crop, irrigation with low-salinity water is applied to the field to leach undesirable salts from the upper portion of the soil profile to provide an environment suitable for the growth of the subsequent salt-sensitive crop. The serial strategy is executed by developing (1) crop rotation plan that can make best use of the available low and high electrolyte waters and (2) an irrigation plan for the entire crop rotation duration that can be based on crop tolerance against irrigation water salinity, sodicity and salt sensitivity of the selected crops at different growth stages. Field studies conducted in several areas of the world involving the cyclic re-use of salinedrainage water for irrigation have demonstrated that this strategy is sustainable on a broad range of soils, provided the problems of soil crusting, poor aeration and tilth are dealt with optimum management.

The reuse of drainage water in SBC system is an attractive management option that has been proposed for many irrigated agricultural areas. Crop suitability for reuse system depends on the influence of $NaSO_4$ dominated water on biomass production, plant sustainability and mineral elements that are critically important for forage quality. The implementation of the drainage water reuse system requires sustainable cropping system, which incorporated useful salt tolerant agronomic species.

The SBC systems for the management of drainage effluent are unlikely to function effectively in areas with deep water table levels and/or deep, permeable profiles underlain by aquifers. Large components of the leachate can by-pass the tile drains and escape to greater depths in the profile, thus making the systems operate poorly (Jury *et al.*, 2003). According to Ninghu *et al.* (2005), a suitable site for SBC (in terms of soil profile) must be in a place where tile drains are installed on top of an impermeable barrier at relatively shallow depth in the profile (about 1-1.5 m below surface).

A field study conducted at red rock ranch where most fields had been irrigated with drainage water for five to six years and the soils were in poor physical condition. In that study, tall wheat grass grew well under highly saline conditions (18-20 dS m^{-1} of EC_e), as well as creeping wild rye (*Leymus triticoides* var. 'Rio') in a field with lower salinity. Salt tolerant alfalfa cultivars (*Medicago sativum*, mix of vars. 'Salado' and '801S') also grew well and forage quality was very high, but only under irrigation with non-saline or blended drainage water resulting in soil salinity less than 7 dS m^{-1} of EC_e.

Banuelos and Lin (2006) conducted multi year fieldstudy and concluded as, the plant species *viz., Helianthus annuus, Lactuca sativa, Lycopersicon esculentum, Gossypiumhirsutum, Medicago sativa, Brassica napus, Distichlis spicata* and *Salicornia bigeloviigrew* well under drainage water reuse system. The quality of drainage water decreased along the waterreuse path, with a sulphate dominated salinity change from, EC 4.5to 15.2 dS m^{-1}; soluble boron from 3.4 to 14.5 mg L^{-1} and solubleSe from 0.08 to 1.18 mg L^{-1}. Soil salinity and concentrationof boron and Se increased with decreasing quality of reused drainagewater.

4. Impact of saline drainage water irrigation on soil and crops

The sustainability of irrigated agriculture with saline water is a real challenge. Saline water irrigation creates salts stress in soil. High amount of soluble salts in irrigation water or in soil do not have adverse impacts on soil structure and hydraulic properties. Rather, saline conditions may have favorable effects on soil structure, development and stability. The adverse effects of salinity on crop growth from two aspects, *i.e* increasing the osmotic pressure and thereby making the water in the soil less available for the plants, and specific effects of some elements or ions present in excess concentration. In addition, the imbalances and induced deficiencies in plant available nutrients in salt affected soil may affect the plant growth adversely.

In semi-arid zones evaporation tends to accumulate salts in the upper soil profile, especially when it is associated with an insufficient leaching or where soluble salts move upward in the soil profile from water table instead of downward. Such accumulation of salts in the soil may alter its physical and chemical properties including soil structure and hydraulic conductivity. Excessive amount of exchangeable Na and high pH decrease soil permeability, water holding capacity and infiltration rate through swelling and dispersion of clays. Proper management of saline water and selection of crop would minimize their deleterious effects on soil properties and crop yield.The drainage water could be applied to grow rice and wheat crops without considerable damage to soil health provided the soil is well drained.

The saline drainage water of varying salinity levels can be successfully utilized for irrigating winter wheat without any soil degradation. The EC_e values after the monsoon rain shows that the soil salinity of these soils can be managed satisfactorily for sustained crop yields. However, the extent of salt leaching and crop establishment depends on total amount of monsoon rain and adequate subsurface drainage.

Grattan and Grieve (1999) reported that use of saline-sodic water for irrigation tends to increase soil pH that impact nutrient availability, rendering plants with malnutrition. The saline drainage waters (ECs 6, 9, 12 and 18.8 dS m^{-1}) could be used successfully for 7 years to irrigate different crops without any serious degradation of a coarse-textured soil. The crop rotations were, wheat-fallow for 3 years, and wheat-pearl millet or sorghum for 4 years. The mean yield reduction was approximately 4 per cent when water EC of 6 dS m^{-1} was used for irrigation. The crop yield declined approximately 22 per cent where the EC of 18.8 dS m^{-1} and SAR of 15 water used for irrigation. The soil salinity levels developed by the saline-sodic irrigation water were managed satisfactorily by monsoon rains.

The reuse of drainage water led to significant fluctuations in salinity in the soil surface and throughout the soil profile. Leaching by winter rains had little effect on salinity in lower parts of the soil profile. SAR values for the surface 15 cm of soil also increased relative to initial soil values after irrigation with saline drainage water.

However, the negative aspects of irrigation with saline drainage water includes, increase in soil salinity and boron which can severely reduce plant growth. Furthermore, crops grown in drainage water irrigated fields must be tolerant of soils with hard surface crusts, water-logging and low oxygen in the root zone following irrigation.

When saline water is used as an irrigation source, soil salinity problems can develop as salts accumulate in the root zone and the presence of Na and Cl in groundwater are absorbed by plants and accumulate in the leaves. This may result in reduced plant growth and yields. Excess cations such as bicarbonate and chloride present in irrigation water, increased the soil pH, EC and ESP.Higher concentration of Na and Cl in irrigation water may also interfere with pasture's ability to uptake nutrients such as K, Mg, N and P, all of which are essential for healthy crop growth.

Saline water reduces crop growth and sodicity can adversely affect soil structure thereby indirectly affecting plant growth by poor soil aeration and increased surface crust formation.Under saline drainage water reuse systems, soil salinity and concentrationof "B" and "Se" increased with decreasing quality of reused drainagewater.

On the basis of changes in soil ECe and SAR under different irrigation and soil management options on a sandy loam nonsaline-nonsodic soil, concluded that irrigation with saline-sodic water without appropriate management could cause deterioration in physical and chemical properties of good arable soils. However, saline-sodic water could be used without negative effects on soil quality or crop yields (over a 3-year period) if it was used within a management approach that included alternative irrigations with freshwater or appropriate soil amendments (Murtaza *et al.*, 2006).

5. Impact of amendment application on soil and crops

A soil amendment is any material added to soil to improve its physical properties, fertility, health, plant growth and yield. Addition of organic manures (Poultry manure, farm yard manure, *Sesbania* and *Gliricidia*) to soil enhances soil organic status and microbial activity/diversity, which subsequently enhance soil enzyme synthesis and accumulation. Green manuring, use of farm yard manure, use of pressmud, effective microorganism technology, now a days has become important in maintaining soil fertility.

One of the important effects of adding organic matter in soil is to increase water retention capacity which is due to reduced bulk density, increased porosity and increased specific surface area of soil particles. The addition of organic fertilizers improved the soil physical and biological properties, mineral fertilizer apparently induced a similar effect in the soil because it caused an increase in soil porosity, shrinkage and enzyme activity. In addition to structural improvements, incorporation of organic/ green manures have added advantages in soils irrigated with saline water in several ways. Because of the sensitivity of the nitrification process to salinity, losses through NH_3, volatilization is aggravated. Thus, the manure can serve as a temporary bonding agent for the ammonical pool of N and reduce losses. Organic matter inputs through organic amendment, in addition to supplying nutrients, improve soil aggregation and stimulate microbial diversity and activity.

(i) Impact of gypsum on soil and crop

The adverse effects of high Na on the physical and chemical properties of soils can be mitigated by use of gypsum, which contains 23 per cent of Ca. Gypsum application improves soil structure in heavy textured soil, so that water infiltration and the ability of roots to penetrate the soil are enhanced. The most common method for maintaining water infiltration is tillage and gypsum incorporation into the soil, often at rates from 2-4 t ha^{-1}. For amelioration of fine textured saline sodic soils, higher quantity of water and gypsum along with organic amendments needed than normally recommended.

Addition of gypsum showed a yield increase of 15 per cent in wheat (*Triticum vulgare*)and sorghum (*Sorghum vulgare*). The ameliorative effect of gypsum (10 and 35 Mg ha^{-1}) on subsoil acidity recorded improved crop yield of both corn (29-50 per cent) and alfalfa (50 per cent). The combined application of FYM and gypsum, found to increase maize yield significantly more compared with FYM and gypsum supplied alone under salt affected soil condition.

The combined application of gypsum, pressmud and farmyard manure followed by pressmud alone or in combination with FYM in yield of rice crop under saline-sodic conditions in Mardan/Swabi districts and gypsum proved the best in reclaiming the soil with regards to pH. Integrated application of recommended dose of fertilizers, FYM and gypsum recorded significantly superior pod yield, NPK uptake and available N, P and K in groundnut crop over control.

(ii) Impact of organic amendments on soil and crops

The quality and value of organic soil amendments are often measured in terms of their contributions to nutrient supplies and soil fertility. However, they can also have significant effect on the microbiological and chemical properties of the soil, which are indirectly responsible for supporting crop growth. In particular, the microbiological properties of soil can influence soil organic matter decomposition and soil enzymatic activities.

Application of organic manures had positive and significant influence on the fertility status of soil. The organic carbon content was significantly higher in the treatments that received organic manures. The availability of zinc and iron was increased by the incorporation of organic manures with no effect on the availability of manganese and copper.

Impact of FYM on Soil and Crops

Farmyard manure has a beneficial acidifying effect on the sodicity of the soil both through the action of organic acids formed during its breakdown and because the Ca and Mg in FYM replaces the Na from the exchange complex. Therefore, addition of organic materials would help in the reclamation process by reducing pH and exchangeable Na in soils. Because of small and less active microflora in saline soils, mineralisation of organic nutrient fractions is comparatively low. So the retention of nutrients in organic forms for longer periods will guard against their leaching and other losses.

The role of FYM is multidimensional ranging from building up of organic matter, maintaining favorable soil physical properties and balanced supply of nutrients. Application of FYM not only improved the physico-chemical properties of the soil like bulk density, water holding capacity and organic carbon content but also had little effect on residual P and K in the soil.

Green manuring and FYM incorporation increased the water stable aggregates, infiltration rate and reduced the bulk density of soil and helped to improve the physical conditions. Application of FYM and vermicompost decreased the bulk density and increased the water holding capacity than NPK application.

Addition of FYM (or) pressmud @ 15 t ha^{-1} and green manure (*Crotalaria juncea*) slightlyincreased the organic carbon, total N and available P, K, S content of soil and it reduced 25 per cent of inorganic fertilizer application. Application of FYM and vermicompost increased the soil microbial population. The organic manure produced more microbial biomass than inorganic and increased the proportion of labile carbon and N by directly stimulating the activity of the microorganisms.The FYM acts directly by increasing the crop yield either by accelerating the respiratory process through cell permeability or by hormone growth action. It supplies N, P and S in available forms to the plants through microbial decomposition.

A positive influence of FYM was recorded on rice plant height, number of tillers hill^{-1} and dry matter production with increased yield attributes and yield. Addition of FYM @ 12.5 t ha^{-1} + *Azospirillum* @ 2 kg ha^{-1} increased the productive tiller m^{-2}, filled grains per panicle, panicle length, finally grain yield and straw yield of rice. The growth and yield of maize were increased significantly with the application of enriched FYM.

Sharma and Misra (1997) reported an enhancement in yield, water use efficiency, uptake of nutrients and protein yield in soybean due to combined use of FYM and reduced level of fertilizer. The application of FYM @ 5 and 10 t ha^{-1} significantly increased the growth, yield attributes and quality of sunflower. Application of FYM and composted coir pith recorded the highest seed and stalk yield of *Sesamum*.

Impact of Vermicompost on Soil and Crop

Use of vermicastings as biofertilizer can be one of the measures to overcome productivity crisis in agriculture and play a multifaceted role in the improvement in soil texture through its influence on soil pH, as agent of physical decomposition by promoting humus formation, by improving soil texture and its enrichment.

Significant reduction, in bulk density was observed in treatment that received vermicompost (5 t ha^{-1}) along with chemical fertilizers than chemical fertilizers alone in rice field. Application of vermicompost @ 5 t ha^{-1} significantly increased organic carbon in soil. Application of 50 per cent recommended dose of N through vermicompost + 50 per cent through urea improved the soil fertility. Application of vermicompost @ 5 (or) 10 t ha^{-1} in strawberries increased the dehydrogenase activity and microbial biomass – N, increased amounts of NH_4 – N, NO_3-N and orthophosphates of soil.

The increase in yield of rice with the application of vermicompost @ 5 t ha^{-1} along with recommended dose of NPK. Sharma *et al.* (2005) reported that the highest yield in wheat crop when vermicompost was applied with recommended dose of NPK. Dry fodder yield (7.51 t ha^{-1}) of maize and total N (171.67 kg ha^{-1}) and P (28.61 kg ha^{-1}) uptake by the chickpea - maize cropping system also increased significantly with the application of vermicompost to chick pea.Significant increase in nutrient content in plant biomass was observed in greengram by vermicompost application @ 5 t ha^{-1}. Vermicompost application significantly increased plant height, leaf area index and grain yield in soybean crop.

Application of vermicompost@ 10 t ha^{-1} has increased plant height, number of leaves per plant, leaf area, bulb length, diameter, weight and yield of onion. The highest soil organic carbon was recorded in the vermicompost and pressmud treated with *Sesbania* as intercrop under sugarcane field soil.

Impact of Biocompost on Soil and Crops

The use of compost can improve the physical, chemical and microbiological characteristics of cultivated soil, reduces the water requirement for plant growth by increasing the availability of moisture and increase the crop production.Application of 50 per cent NPK + biocompost @ 10 t ha^{-1} increased the available N, P, K and S. Addition of paper mill waste compost at the rate of 5 to 10 t ha^{-1} improved soil biological activity. The increased availability of nutrients by the application of paper mill solid waste biomanure. The paper board mill treated effluent irrigation along with biocompost increased the vegetable cowpea yield upto 28 per cent when compared with normal farmers practice.

The pod yield of groundnut cultivated under biocompost, prepared by mixing bagasse pith, activated sludge and ETP sludge at 2:1:1 ratio was comparable with the yield obtained from the crop cultivated under FYM application. The treated TNPL effluent irrigation resulted in higher pod yield than well water irrigation in groundnut crop under biocompost application (Udayasoorian *et al.*, 2004).

Impact of Pressmud on Soil and Crop

The application of green manure, pressmud or cow dung brought some increase in soil organic matter. Application of pressmud @ 12.5 t ha^{-1} significantly improved soil organic carbon, pH, EC and soil bacteria, fungi, actinomycetes population and enhanced the soil fertility status. The integrated use of pressmud @ 5 t ha^{-1} along with mineral nutrition of NPK at recommended dose had appreciably enhanced the availability of P, K, Ca, Fe, Zn and activity of phosphatase enzyme and population of actinomycetes under sugarcane.

Application of pressmud compost at the rate of 10 t ha^{-1} increased the maize and wheat yield by 129.4 and 62.2 per cent, respectively. The yield of maize and oil seed crops were higher when amended with pressmud. Addition of pressmud and continuous effluent irrigation was reported to be advantageous to fodder grass ecosystem as compared to that of seasonal crops.

6. Impact of saline water irrigation with amendments on soil and crops

Recycling and reuse of wastewater in agriculture is not only helpful for conserving the plant nutrients and water for irrigation but also offers a low cost technology for the disposal of wastewater from the view point of environmental pollution abatement (Figure 2.2).

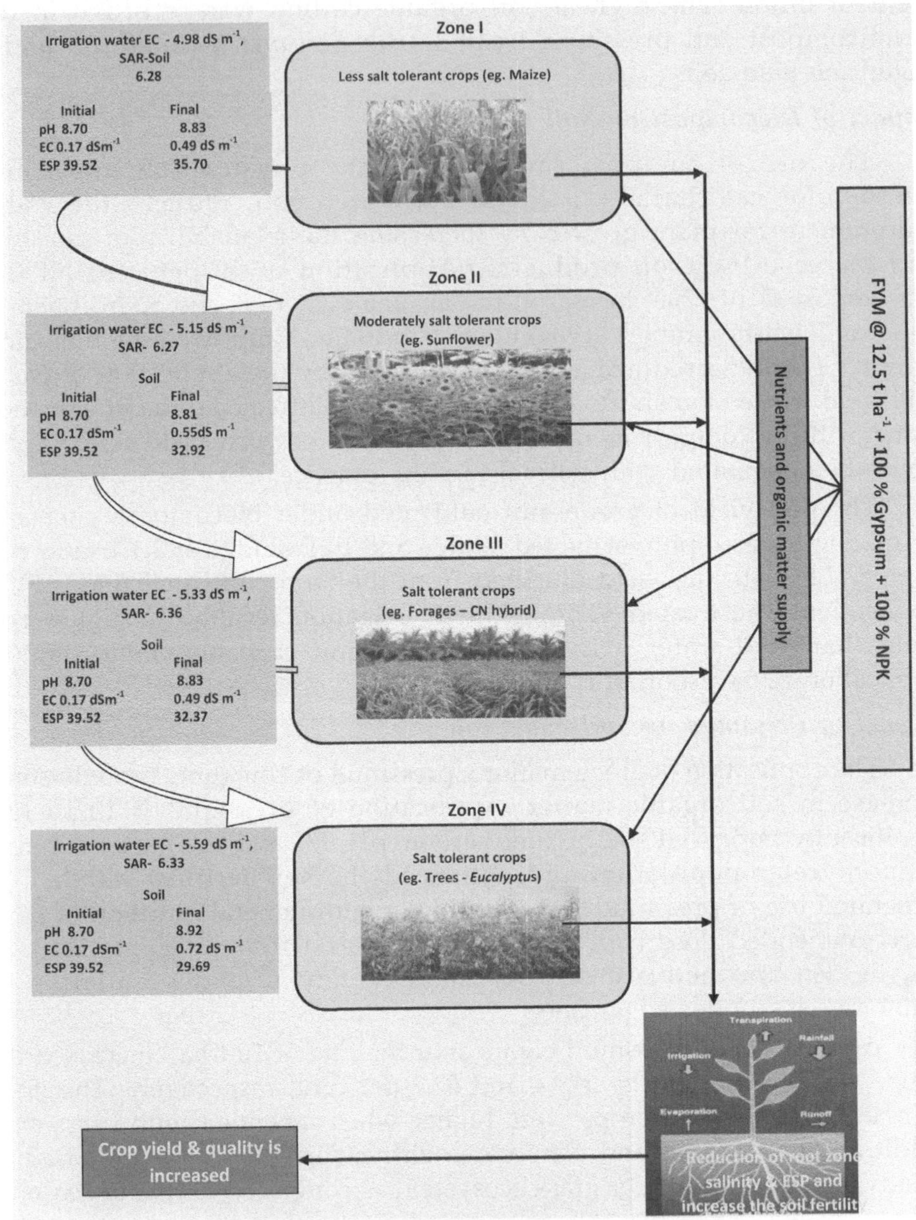

Fig. 2.2: Schematic representation of agricultural drainage water management through SBC system

The use of poor quality drainage water for irrigation without proper amendments should be discouraged as it can increase soil salinity. The use of biocompost is recommended in case of irrigation with saline drainage water (Taalab *et al.*, 2008). The usage of gypsum can mitigate negative impact on soil physical properties under saline-sodic drainage water to irrigate salt-tolerant, perennial grasses.

Irrigation with saline-sodic water together with amendments significantly increased infiltration rate than saline-sodic water alone, where bulk density was increased in cotton-wheat rotation. Incorporation of organic materials for reducing deleterious effects of poor quality irrigation water is through mobilization of native soil Ca from $CaCO_3$ and other Ca bearing minerals.

Application of gypsum and cover crop incorporation may improve soil physicalproperties in cyclic saline drainage water reuse system, but these improvements do not necessarily correlate with higher crop stands and yields. Application of gypsum, FYM/pressmud along with recommended dose of fertilizers must be used to sustain the productivity of rice-wheat system in areas having sodic ground water for irrigation.

Pure drainage water irrigation without any amendment reduced wheat grain yield by 1433 kg ha^{-1} (39 per cent). Addition of gypsum @ 25 per cent gypsum requirement reduced the yield loss to 972 kg ha^{-1} (27 per cent) under drainage water irrigation.

Oil content and crude protein content of groundnut crop were increased due to addition of composted bagasse pith manure and treated TNPL effluent irrigation (Udayasoorian *et al.*, 2004). The sustainable cane and sugarcane yields with good quality juice can be obtained by applying gypsum/FYM or both under sodic and only FYM under saline – sodic water irrigation. Addition of solid wastes and continuous effluent irrigation were reported to be advantageous to fodder grass ecosystem.

7. Protective mechanisms of plants under salinity

An important consequence of salinity stress in plants is the excessive generation of Reactive Oxygen Species (ROS) such as super oxide anion (O_2^-), H_2O_2 and the hydroxyl radicals (OH^-) particularly in chloroplast and mitochondria. Generation of ROS such as super oxide, H_2O_2 and hydroxyl molecules causes rapid cell damage. Plants under stress produce some defense mechanisms to protect themselves from the harmful effect of oxidative stress. ROS scavenging is one of the common defense responses against abiotic stresses. The major ROS scavenging activities include complex non-enzymatic (ascorbate, glutathione, a-tocopherol) and enzymatic responses includes Catalase (CAT), Ascorbate Peroxidase (APX), Glutathione Reductase (GR), Super Oxide Dismutase (SOD) etc., and stress proteins (proline and glycinebetaine). Antioxidant mechanisms may provide a strategy to enhance salt tolerance in plants.

Antioxidant enzymes

Peroxidase activity showes marginal change at lower salinity level in both leaves and roots indicating certain degree of adjustment by plants to adverse condition. The increased peroxidase and super oxide dismutase activity become useful for adaptation under conditions requiring prevention of peroxidation of membrane lipids. Higher peroxidase activity particularly in tolerant cultivar is an indication to prevent degradation of membrane integrity of the cells against free radicals formed under salt stress in rice varieties.

The activity of antioxidant enzymes was reported to increase under saline conditions in shoot cultures of rice and wheat shoot, but decreased in wheat roots or was unaffected as in the case of SOD in cucumber. Higher enzyme activity was observed under saline conditions mainly in the roots of maize and sunflower, in contrast to the results of Meneguzzo *et al.* (1999) who described an increase in the antioxidant enzyme activities in the shoots of durum wheat and decrease in its roots.

Transgenic plants over expressing ROS scavenging enzymes, such as ascorbate peroxidase glutathione S-transferase/glutathione peroxidase and SOD showed increased levels of tolerance to osmotic and oxidative stresses.

High salinity reduced SOD activity in both roots (28 per cent in high salinity) and in leaves (16 per cent at low and 38 per cent at high salinity) of *Catharanthus roseus*, but low salinity led to an increase in root SOD activity upto 2.85 per cent. In leaves, the peroxidase activity decreased under salinity and in roots it showed a slight increase of up to 10 per cent in low salinity and a 29 per cent decrease in high salinity when compared to control plants.

Proline

During osmotic stress, plant cells accumulate low molecular weight osmolytes to prevent water loss and maintain turgor. High level synthesis of osmoprotectants and the key genes encoding enzymes are leading to increased proline accumulation. Proline serves as a storage sink for carbon, N and a free-radical scavenger. It also stabilizes sub cellular structures and buffers cellular redox potential under stress and hence, proline is known as osmoprotectants. Due to salt treatment significant accumulation of proline was observed, in groundnut. Proline content increased with increasing salt concentration in sunflower. Proline content was highest in the presence of NaCl in both cotyledons and the embryonic axis of peanut seedlings.

The proline content of the roots was increased by treatment with NaCl for two weeks, but the increment was lower than that in the shoots. Further increases in the duration of NaCl treatment beyond two weeks did not result in an appreciable increase in proline content in the shoots or roots in casuarina.

8. Effect of saline water irrigation on groundwater quality

The drainage water contains huge quantity of salts mostly in dissolved form. Due to rain water and/or irrigation water, these salts and nutrients leach down in the soil profile and contaminate the groundwater. Though leaching of salts are essential for crop growth its potential in contaminating the groundwater can not be ignored. Without leaching, salts accumulate in direct proportion to the salt loading of the drainage water. The major effect of wastewater disposal on land is the possibility of groundwater pollution and mobility of metals depending upon soil conditions and applied dose etc. leaching of inorganic pollutants such as chlorides, sulphates, nitrates and metals take place during the process.

Valliappan (1998) reported that pH of the soil was found significantly increased due to leaching in both the saline and non- saline sodic soil and he also reported that the SAR and ESP of the soil were reduced after two leaching from 10.15 to 3.16 and from 44.02 to 27.40, respectively.

The quality parameters of groundwater *viz.*, pH, EC, total hardness, CO_3, HCO_3, Cl, SO_4, Ca, Mg and K content of groundwater in and around the Bipco factory site, Thekkampatti, Tamil Nadu also increased due to continuous discharge of treated effluent for irrigation. Groundwater within the wastewater irrigated areas had less pH but high EC, total hardness, CO_3, HCO_3, Cl, SO_4, Na, Ca, Mg, K, per cent Na, SAR and RSC than that of river Cauvery basins. The EC and SAR values increased two to three times within four years of continuous effluent irrigation (Udayasoorian and Prabu, 2005).

9. Role of halophilic bacteria on crops under salinity

Microbial process in the soil

Soil microbial biomass constituents both a labile sink and source of plant nutrients, which is a pool of nutrients that is easily remobilized. Microbial community composed of metabolically diverse biocatalysts with key roles in soil nutrient cycling. Microbial biomass has been described important roles in soil as a nutrient pool, driving force of nutrient turnover and early indicator of soil/ crop management.

Plant Growth Promoting Rhizobacteria (PGPR)

Kloepper and Schroth (1981) for the first time reported that specific rhizosphere bacteria applied to seeds could colonize roots and promote plant growth which was later called as Plant Growth Promoting Rhizobacteria (PGPR). Halotolerant/Halophilic bacteria are being utilized in plant-bacteria interaction, because they could flourish in hyper saline conditions and interacting with plants may restore these lands to productivity.

Rhizosphere bacteria improve the uptake of nutrients by plants and/ or produce plant growth promoting compounds and regenerate the quality of soil. They also protect plant root surfaces from colonization by pathogenic microbes through direct competitive effects and production of antimicrobial agents. Bacteria from different sources could promote seedling growth under saline conditions. Stimulated seedling growth was described to the decreased uptake of Na^+ or increased auxin level in the cells accompanied by decreased Na^+uptake.Studies carried out on application of mixtures of halotolerant bacteria revealed that inoculation significantly increased plant height, fresh weight and dry weight under salt stressed conditions.

Inoculation of oil seed halophyte *Salicornia bigelovi* with different mixtures *i.e* mixture of *Vibrio aestuarians* with *Vibrio proteolyticus* and *Phyllobacterium myrsinacearum* combined with *Bacillus licheniformis*, enhanced plant growth and increased the N, protein and fatty acid content of the seeds.

A considerable number of bacterial species associated with the plant rhizosphere such as *Bacillus, Pseudomonas, Azospirillum, Anthrobacter* and *Acinetobacter* are able to exert a beneficial effect upon plant growth. These bacteria are known to improve solubilization of fixed soil P and applied phosphates resulting in higher crop yields. Phosphate solubilization ability of these bacteria were higher than control in presence of 10 per cent salts (NaCl, $CaCl_2$ and KCl).

Wokitke *et al.* (2004) observed that the gram positive bacteria *Bacillus subtilis* is known to positively influence plant growth, vitality and ability of the plant to cope with pathogens often resulting in higher yields. These beneficial effects are documented in field crops, where it has been ascribed to a biotic stress they observed vegetative plant growth of tomato was improved significantly due to the inoculation with *B. subtilis* compared with control under salinity level of EC 4 dS m^{-1}.

Total green dry matter yield as well as root dry weight of *Trifolium alesxandrium* decreased consecutively with increase in salinity levels (8, 12 and 16 dS m^{-1}), while *Rhizobium* inoculation created a positive effect and these parameters remained significantly higher than the similar levels without inoculation. Hamida *et al.* (2004) found that the inoculation with *Azospirillum* (growth promoting rhizobacteria) of salt stressed maize, markedly altered the selectivity of Na^+, K^+ and Ca^{++} also the proline declined significantly comparing with control.

Al-Abed *et al.* (2004) reported that the TRX-30 catalyst aerobic bacteria were very efficient in reducing the EC_e values of saline soils in the first week of application by almost 50 per cent. The microbial activity was responsible for modifying the salts and minerals into usable and inert compounds in the soil matrix.

The water conservation through recycling of waste water is a most important phenomenon. In this context, recycling of drainage water by using SBC system is an innovative technology for adoption.

REFERENCES

Al-Abed, N., J. Amayreh, A. Al-Afifi and G. Al-Hiyari. 2004. Bioremediation of a Jordanian Saline Soil: A Laboratory Study. Commun. Soil Sci. Plant Anal., 35: 1467-1469.

Banuelos, G.S and Z.Q. Lin. 2006. Reuse of Agricultural Drainage Water in Central California: Phytosustainability in Soil with High Levels of Salinity and Toxic Trace Elements. *Geological Society, London, Special Publications,* 266: 79-88.

Grattan, S.R and C.M. Grieve. 1999. Salinity - mineral Nutrient Relations in Horticultural Crops. Hort. Sci., 78: 127-157.

Hamida, M.A.E.S., M.A.K. Shaddad and M.M. Doaa. 2004. Mechanisms of Salt Tolerance and Interactive Effects of *Azospirillum brasillens* Inoculation on Maize Cultivars Grown under Salt Stress Conditions. Plant Growth Regul., 44: 165-174.

Kloepper, J.W and M.N. Schroth. 1981. Development of a Powder Formulation of Rhizobacteria for Inoculation of Potato Seed Pieces. Phytopathology,71: 590-592.

Meneguzzo, S., F. Navari-Izzo and R. Izzo. 1999. Antioxidative Responses of Shoots and Roots of Wheat to Increasing NaCl Concentrations. J. Plant Physiol., 155: 274-80.

Murtaza, G., A. Ghafoor and M. Qadir. 2006. Irrigation and Soil Management Strategies for using Saline-sodic Water in a Cotton–Wheat Rotation. Agric. Water Manage., 81: 98-114.

Ninghu, S.U., M. Bethune, L. Mann and A. Heuperman. 2005. Simulating Water and Salt Movement in Tile-drained Fields Irrigated with Saline Water under a Serial Biological Concentration Management Scenario. Agric. Water Manage., 78: 165-180.

Oster, J.D and D.E. Birkle. 2001. Potential Crop Production Systems using Saline Irrigation Waters. In: Proc. of Intl. Seminar on Prospects of Saline Agriculture in the GCC Countries, March 18-20, Dubai, United Arab Emirates.

Sharma, B.R and P.S. Minhas. 2005. Strategies for Managing Saline/Alkali Waters for Sustainable Agricultural Production in South Asia. Agric. Water Manage., 78: 136-151.

Sharma, D.P and K.V.G.K. Rao. 1998. Strategy for Long Term use of Saline Drainage Water for Irrigation in Semi-arid Regions. Soil Till. Res., 48: 287-295.

Sharma, D.P. 2007. Reuse Potential of Drainage Effluents. In: Natl. Level Training Course on Land Drainage for Reclamation of Water Logged Saline Lands (Eds.) S.K. Ambast, S.K.Gupta and S. Gurbachan. February 19-25, Karnal, India, pp. 190-200.

Sharma, K., S. Kamala and S.P. Dev. 2005. Efficacy of Vermicompost for Improving Crop yield and Nutrient uptake in Wheat. J. Soils Crops, 15: 269-273.

Sharma, R.A and O.R. Misra. 1997. Crop Residues, FYM and Fertilizer use in Relation to Growth, yield and Nutrient uptake by Soybean. Crop Res., 13: 51-57.

Taalab, S., E. Okasha and A.H. Ali. 2008. Influence of Saline Irrigation Water and Composted Tomato Residues on yield and Nutrient uptake of Beet Root Grown on Sandy Loamy Soil. Res. J. Agric. Biol. Sci., 4: 219-227.

Tanji, K.K and F.F. Karajeh. 1993. Saline Drain Water Reuse in Agroforestry Systems. J. Irrig. Drain. Eng., 119: 170-180.

Udayasoorian, C and P.C. Prabu. 2005. Reclamation of Paper Mill Effluent Polluted Saline Sodic Soil Habitat using Native Cyanobacteria *Westiellopsis*. In: Pulp and Paper Conference. Hilton Kuala Lumpur, Malaysia, p. 33.

Udayasoorian, C., P.C. Prabu and K. Mini. 2004. Influence of Composted Bagasse Pith and Treated Paper Mill Effluent Irrigation on Groundnut. Madras Agric. J., 91: 126-129.

Valliappan, K. 1998. Recycling of Distillery Spentwash - An Eco-friendly Effective Reclamation Technology for Sodic Soils. Ph.D. Thesis, Tamil Nadu Agric. Univ., Coimbatore, India.

Wokitke, M., A. Hanafi and W.H. Schnitzler. 2004. Effect of Salinity and *Bacillus subtilis* on Whitefly (*Trialeurodes vaporariorum,*) in Hydroponically Grown Tomatoes (*Lycopersicon esculentum*). Acta Hort., 659: 323-329.

Pages: 37-54

Irrigation Practices and Sustainable Agriculture

Edited by: **Dr. Prasann Kumar and Dr. Pawan Kumar 'Bharti'**

ISBN: 978-93-88854-31-3

Edition: **2020**

Published by: **Discovery Publishing House Pvt. Ltd., New Delhi (India)**

3 Putrescine and Mycorrhiza for Waterlogging Stress in Maize

Prasann Kumar[1,2*], Johnson Yumnam[1]

GRAPHICAL ABSTRACT

Keywords: Crop, Mycorrhiza, Putrescine, Waterlogging

INTRODUCTION

Maize (*Zea mays* L.) is known as the queen of cereals because of its higher genetic yield potential among the cereals. Its probable place of origin lies in Tehuacan valley of Mexico (Lowa St. Univ., 2014). Its chromosome number is 2n=20 and belongs to the family Poaceae. It is a most versatile

[1] Department of Agronomy, School of Agriculture, Lovely Professional University, Jalandhar - 144 411 (Punjab) (India)

[2] Divison of Research and Development,, Lovely Professional University, Jalandhar - 144 411 (Punjab) (India)

emerging crop having wider adaptability to varied agro-climatic conditions. It is grown from 58° N to 40°S, from below sea level to altitudes higher than 3000 m, and in areas with 250 mm to more than 5000 mm of rainfall per year and with a growing cycle ranging from 3 to 13 months (CIMMYT 2000). It is a third important cereal with the highest production and productivity next to wheat and paddy. It is a well-known fact that maize is a heavy feeder for both nutrients and soil moisture as well as also is a high yielding, easy to process, readily digestible and cheaper than other cereals. However, the major maize production areas are located in temperate regions of the globe. The United States, China, Brazil, and Mexico account for 70% of global production. India has 5% of corn acreage and contributes 2% of world production.In India, about 28% of maize produced is used for food purpose, about 11% as livestock feed, 48% as poultry feed, 12% in wet milling industry (for example starch and oil production) and 1% as seed (AICRP on Maize, 2007). In the last one decade, it has registered the highest growth rate among all food grains including wheat and rice because of newly emerging food habits as well as enhanced industrial requirement (Andersene and Kupper H. 2013). Maize is an important multipurpose cereal crop used as food, feed, fodder, fuel and in the manufacture of industrial product. Generally, maize kernels are used either for food or feed for livestock (Anda, 2011, Ardnini 2004). The grains are rich in vitamin viz., A, C and E, carbohydrates, essential minerals and protein viz., zein, which is a class of prolamine protein. In addition to staple food for human being and quality feed for animals, maize serves as a basic raw material and as an ingredient to thousands of industrial products that includes starch, oil, protein, alcoholic beverages, food sweeteners, pharmaceutical, cosmetic, film, textile, gum, package and paper industries, etc. Maize is grown in about 166 countries occupying 165 m ha area with the production of more than 800 m t and a productivity of 5.1 t ha^{-1}. In India maize has higher growth rate among food crops contributing 5 percent area, 2.4 percent production to world maize. Maize production in India was around 23 Million tonnes in 2013-14. The area under maize cultivation was around 9.4 Million hectares in 2013-14, which accounts nearly 9 percent to the national food basket and more than 155 billion to the agricultural GDP (Azizian *et al.*, 2013. The terms "water-logged" is used to refer to the type of soil that is saturated with water and thus no longer have the ability to keep oxygen between its particles. Blockage of water on the land surface, especially in a low-lying area is the main causes to enhance water-logged conditions. The geology, topography, drainage, and the amount of water supplied to the site controlled the blocking of water. Changing land use patterns is also the result of changing land within the human environment. Sometimes the outcome of all-round embanking with poor drainage system is also responsible to to create a water-logged situation of an area. Water-logging happens due to unscientific management of water as well as obstruction of natural drainage systems by the hazard embankment construction through the disturbance of the balance inflow and outflow of water. Damage to agricultural lands affecting the crops and thus the livelihood and the economy of the country is caused by the waterlogging like flooding. The water-logged situation in both the rural and urban areas can be created within a very short period of time with excessive rainfall. In India, land degradation is one ofthe most problem which is the main reasons of water-logging. Thus, different factors like geological structure, excessive rainfall, drainage congestion, dense haphazard embankments, cyclones, flooding, river basin encroachment through siltation, and finally human activities have resulted to enhance the water-logged situation.

WATERLOGGING AND WATER TABLE

Furthermore, irrigation may cause water-logging. Rising water table within the subsurface soil is one of the consequences which is regarded as water-logging. It is the combination of all-round intro and interrelationship of climatic, geomorphic, hydrologic, vegetative, and anthropogenic factors in our environment. Some of the water-logging scenarios are permanent and others are manifested as seasonal. Thus water-logging is time and place specifically as well. Water-logged areas cannot be always considered as wetlands, but sometimes they are manifested as wetlands. When water-logging incidence is created, it can be easily observed as well as studied from the environment perspective. Depends upon the type of crop, soil and quantity of water determine the water table which can be considered as harmful. With extent more in fine soils than coarse soils, the height of the capillary fringe in soils shows variation from 0.9 to 1.5m. Hence, during monsoon, water table which are remains within 1.5m from the surface are prone to be water-logged. As per Central Ground Water Board, the areas with water table within 2m below ground level are considered as prone to waterlogging and critical level is 2-3 below the ground level.

POLYAMINES: AN ORGANIC COMPOUNDS

A polyamine is an organic compound having two or more primary amino groups-NH_2. They are also known as a group of natural compounds with an aliphatic nitrogen structure present in almost all living organisms. It plays an important role in many physiological processes such as cell growth and development. Polyamines which are commonly found are putrescine. Spermidine, spermine, etc. the diamine putrescine, the triamine spermidine and the tetraminespermine are ubiquitously found in plant cells while other polyamines are of more limited occurrence. Polyamine metabolism is regulated by the activity of the enzyme ornithine decarboxylase. Polyamine can also be synthesized from the aminoacid arginine and methionine. Polyamines including putrescine are small ubiquitous nitrogenous compounds which are involved in several plant growth and developmental processes (Farooq *et al.*, 2009). They are the recent additions to the class of plant growth regulators, and also considered as a secondary messenger in signaling pathways (Kusano *et al.*, 2008). Polyamines are involved in abiotic stress tolerance in plants (Nayyer *et al.*, 2005). Increased polyamines level in stressed plants is of adaptive significance because of their involvement in the regulation of the cellular ionic environment, maintenance of membrane integrity, prevention of chlorophyll loss, and stimulation of protein, nucleic acid and protective alkaloids (Sharma, 1999). Interaction of polyamines with membrane phospholipids implicates membrane stability under stress conditions (Roberts *et al.*, 1986). Polyamines also protect membranes from oxidative damages as they as free radical scavengers (Besford *et al.*, 1993). Putrescine or tetramethylenediamine, $NH_2(CH_2)_4NH_2$ is related to cadaverine which is produced by the breakdown of amino acids in living and dead organisms and it is toxic when applied in large doses. They are also found in semen and some micro-algae, together with related molecules like spermine and spermidine. Putresicine is made from acrylonitrile (2-propenenitrile) and hydrogen cyanide. This two molecules are reacted together to make succinonitrile, which is similar to putrescine but contain fewer hydrogen atom. And then hydrogenation turns them colorless waxy solid form from succinonitrile into the foul-smelling putrescine. It is found that foliar application of putrescine at 200 ppm significantly increased plant height as well as number of leaves/plant, fresh and dry weight of leaves/plant and highest values of chlorophyll a, chlorophyll b, carotenoids, and soluble sugars content compared with untreated plants on maize crops. The best results were found when plants treated with 200 ppm putrescine.Mycorrhiza is a fungus having a symbiotic or mutualistic relationship with the rhizosphere or roots of the plants. They share a mutualistic relationship in which the mycorrhiza forms a network of filaments that associates with the plant roots which helps them in up taking the mineral nutrients or water while the mycorrhiza is benefitted by getting access to carbohydrates such as glucose and sucrose. The carbohydrates are translocated from their source to root tissues and onto the plant fungal partners. Some plant roots may be unable to uptake nutrients that are chemically or physically immobilized. For example, phosphate ions. Progress in the field of mycorrhiza application is slow because in pure culture, it is difficult to isolate the fungal component. Only Scott Barett (2003) has reported the successful isolation in pure culture (endogen-type) of rhisophagus endophytes and mycorrhiza is synthesis with them.

MYCORRHIZA, AGRICULTURE AND ECOLOGICAL SYSTEM

Mycorrhiza is associated with both agricultural and ecological systems had been widely recognized. The increased plant growth by VAM (vascular avuncular mycorrhiza) association is usually due to increased mineral elements uptake by the hyphae from the soil. Olawuyi *et al.*, 2012, improved water relations and pest resistance of host plants, plants tolerance to a variety of abiotic stresses, increased resistance to soil pathogens. Mycorrhizae can also resist drought in many plants under stress conditions, therefore, the plants infected with VA mycorrhizae are less likely to wilt under drought affected conditions.VAM (vascular arbuscular mycorrhiza) application on maize crops performance was related directly or indirectly to yield of the maize grain as well as colonization of roots had a positive effect on the performance of maize. VAM is one of the most essential factors that determines the success of cover crop rotational systems. Encouraging VAM can potentially benefit cover cropping systems. Therefore, it is imperative to consider VAM associations and crop phenology when making management decisions (Higo M, 2018). Colonization of plant roots by vesicular-arbuscularmycorrhizal fungi is known to be reduced the application of phosphorus since the nutrition of phosphorus is increased in the plants. Hence, It is generally accepted that the concentration of P in the plant rather than the soil regulates VAM colonization. Though the shoot Phosphorus concentration or the mean phosphorus concentration in the root systems and concentration in the specific roots system is not known, but it is of agronomic significance because fertilizer Phosphorus is applied frequently in concentrated zones which are expected to get the result in higher concentration of Phosphorus in roots growing in the fertilized zone as the remainder of the root system.

REVIEW OF LITERATURE CONCERNED WITH PUTRESCINE, MYCORRHIZA AND WATERLOGGING

Panozzo, (2019) has reported that root parameters (length, area, biomass) were more impaired by waterlogging than shoot parameter (shoot height and biomass.) in commercial hybrids and inbred line B-73, with the aim of investigating the current variability in cultivated hybrids and identifying useful morphological and molecular marker for screening tolerant genotypes. Salah (2019) has reported that Compared with WL treatment, application of GABA significantly increased aboveground and root dry matter by 19.0% and 61.0%, promoted photosynthetic rate and chlorophyll content by 19.8% and 36.0%. GABA application was shown to promote the growth of maize seedlings under waterlogging, by down regulating ROIs-producing enzymes, activating antioxidant defense systems, and improving chloroplast ultrastructure and photosynthetic traits. Rafique (2019) has reported that Two-dimensional gel electrophoresis (2DE) was used to examine the protein changes induced by combined stresses, in leaves, of tolerant and susceptible genotypes. He has reported that up-regulated proteins species contributed to maintaining acclimated state and restoring of plant growth and development even under stress. Alternatively, in susceptible genotype, the up-regulated proteins are mainly involved in activation of defense response against the pathogen, and effort to maintain the energy metabolism, and alleviate the genotype to survive under multiple stress condition.Wang F, (2018) has reported that During seedling and silking stages of maize, drought and water logging stresses were introduced respectively to the plants and the results showed that the yield of maize under $S_1T_1D_2$ (straw burying, depth 30cm) treatment in 2016 was significantly increased by 5.7%-7.1%. Compared with all the rest treatments, S1T1D2 treatments (straw burying, depth 30 cm) could significantly promote the growth and spatial distribution of maize root, accounting to release water stress and keep yield stabilization or promotion. Therefore, 30 cm of straw burying could be used as a suitable approach of straw returning for maize production in northeastern China, where the climate is with a pattern of drought first and waterlogging in a later stage. Zang (2018) has reported that waterlogging significantly decreased the maximum green leaf area (GLA) by 10.0~15.3% and 9.3~22.5%, mainly due to the reduction in the below-ear layer leaves at the silking stage in 2014 and 2015, respectively. Thus resulting in a loss of grain yield by 7.0~18.5%. Therefore, this study showed that optimal nitrogen regimes during maize growth are capable of compensating for the impacts caused by waterlogging at the seedling stage. Maestrini, (2018) has reported that he relative performance of areas of a field with a very high wetness index (e.g. depressions) strongly depends on rain patterns because they may be waterlogged in wet years, yielding less than the rest of the field, or wetter during dry years, yielding more than the rest of the field. We show that temporal yield variability is positively correlated ($p < 0.05$) with the probability of observing gleying processes associated with waterlogging for part of the year. These findings shed light on mechanisms underlying temporal variability of yield and can help guide management solutions to increase profit and improve environmental quality. Liang (2018) has reported that favorable alleles of this gene and validated the favorable alleles in two different recombinant inbred line populations. These alleles enhanced waterlogging tolerance in segregating populations, strongly suggesting that GRMZM2G110141 is a key waterlogging tolerance gene. The set of waterlogging tolerance-related genomic regions and associated markers identified here could be valuable for isolating waterlogging tolerance genes and improving this trait in maize. A key candidate gene, GRMZM2G110141, which could be used in marker-assisted selection in maize breeding programs, was detected among the 16 genetic loci associated with waterlogging tolerance identified through genome-wide association study. Du H *et al.* (2017) has reported that six alleles of the 18 originated from the tolerant pool were significantly up-regulated under waterlogging, but not those from the sensitive pool. Importantly, one allele (*GRMZM2G055704*) of the six genes was mapped between umc1619 and umc1948 on chromosome 1 where a QTL associated with waterlogging tolerance was identified in previous research, strongly indicating that *GRMZM2G055704* is a candidate gene responsive to waterlogging. Our research contributes to the knowledge of the molecular mechanism for waterlogging tolerance in maize. In this study, 10 waterlogging sensitive and eight tolerant inbred lines were selected from 60 maize inbred lines with waterlogging response determined and preselected by the International Maize and Wheat Improvement Center (CIMMYT) from over 400 tropical maize inbred lines. Ren (2017) has reported that nitrogen accumulation in each organ and nitrogen allocation proportions in grains decreased significantly after waterlogging, whereas N allocation proportions increased in stem and leaf. The reduction in stem and leaf nitrogen accumulation after waterlogging was mainly caused by a decrease in dry matter accumulation, and a reduction in nitrogen translocation from stems and leaves to grains after waterlogging. Additionally, water-logging decreased the activity of key nitrogen metabolism enzymes (nitrate reductase, glutamine, glutamate synthase, and glutamate dehydrogenase). Khaldun, (2017) has reported that Excess water tolerant hybrid maize varieties could be the better alternative to the farmer increasing the maize production. Considering all the maize yield contributing characters to excess water tolerant parameters Uttaran-2, 900M Gold and Pinaclecan be recommended as less susceptible to excess water stress varieties. Uttaran-2, 900M Gold and Pinacle found capable surviving in the water logged condition. Considering the yield and yield contributing characters Uttaran-2, 900M Gold and Pinacle found promising hybrids and Burirhat could be a good choice for farmers producing summer maize hybrids. Huang, (2017) has reported that Eighteen SNPs (single nucleotide polymorphism) were contained in 18 genes, and eight and nine of 18 genes were responsive to waterlogging stress in tolerant and sensitive lines, respectively. Six alleles of the 18 originated from the tolerant pool were significantly up-regulated under waterlogging. Importantly one allele was mapped and strongly indicated that the gen responsive to waterlogging (GRMZM2G055704). Watnabe (2017) has reported that Discovery of the Z. nicaraguensis chromosomal region responsible for root ROL (radial oxygen loss) barrier formation has improved knowledge of this trait and is an important step towards the improvement of waterlogging tolerance in maize. A radial oxygen loss (ROL) barrier in roots of waterlogging-tolerant plants promotes oxygen movement via aerenchyma to the root tip and impedes soil phytotoxin entry. The molecular mechanism and genetic regulation of ROL barrier formation.Vwioko (2017) has reported that okra and maize tissues respond to the conditions of waterlogging and exogenous ethylene priming by inducing their ethylene biosynthetic genes expressionin order to enhance ethylene production and tolerate the prolonged waterlogging stress. In conclusion, the study revealed that exogenously generated ethylene gas as a priming treatment before or after waterlogging could enhance waterlogging tolereance in maize crops. Arora, (2017) has reported that CWM (Cell wall modification) genes in waterlogging tolerance and these genes can be used as candidates in introgression breeding and genome editing experiments to impart tolerance in maize hybrids. Cell wall modification (CWM) promotes the formation of aerenchyma in roots under waterlogging conditions as an adaptive mechanism. Lysigenousaerenchyma formation in roots improves oxygen transfer in plants, which highlights the importance of CWM as a focal point in waterlogging stress tolerance. Chen (2017) has reported that Native to Ethiopia and often the sustenance for local small farmers, teff thrives in both moisture-stressed and waterlogged soil conditions, making it a dependable staple within and beyond its current center of origin. Today, teff is deemed a healthy wheat alternative in the West and is sought-after by health aficionados and those with coeliac disease or gluten sensitivity. The blooming market for healthy food is breathing new life into this underutilized crop, which has received relatively limited attention from mainstream research perhaps due to its 'orphan crop' status. This review presents the past, present and future of an ancient grain with a potential beyond its size. Emerging evidence suggests that climate change will cause shifts in crop production and yield loss due to more unpredictable and hostile weather patterns. One solution to this problem is through the wider use of underutilized (also called orphan or minor) crops to diversify agricultural systems and food sources. Vwioko, (2017) has reported that okra and maize tissues respond to the conditions of waterlogging and exogenous ethylene priming by inducing their ethylene biosynthetic genes expression in order to enhance ethylene production and tolerate the prolonged waterlogging stress. In conclusion, this study revealed that exogenously generated ethylene gas as a priming treatment before or after waterlogging could enhance waterlogging tolerance in maize and okra crops. Arora *et al*, (2017) have reported that the oxygen transfer in waterlogged roots is promoted by a cross-talk of fermentative, metabolic, and glycolytic pathways that generate ATPs for PCD and aerenchyma formation in root cortical cells. SNPs were mapped to the DEGs regulating aerenchyma formation, ethylene-responsive factors, and glycolysis under stress. RNAseq derived SNPs can be used in selection approaches to breeding tolerant hybrids. Overall, this investigation provided significant evidence of genes operating in the adaptive traits such as ethylene production and aerenchyma formation to cope-up the waterlogging stress. Waterlogging causes yield penalty in maize-growing countries of subtropical regions. Transcriptome analysis of the roots of a tolerant inbred HKI1105 using RNA sequencing revealed differentially expressed genes (DEGs) under waterlogged stress condition. Ren, (2016) has reported that physiological reactions to waterlogging were closely related to lower LAI (leaf area index), chlorophyll content, and Pn (photosynthetic rate) and to the destruction of chloroplast ultrastructure. These negative effects resulted in a decrease in grain yield in response to waterlogging. Summer maize was the most susceptible to damage when waterlogging occurred at V3 (third leaf stage), followed by V6 (sixth leaf stage) and 10VT(10th days after the tasseling stage), with damage increase in the wake of waterlogging duration increasing. Shen (2016), has reported that hese results demonstrate that the exogenous VHb gene confers waterlogging tolerance to the transgenic maize line. In Maize in the place of to the transgenic maize line, the VHb gene is a useful molecular tool for the improvement of waterlogging and submergence-tolerance. Vitreoscilla hemoglobin (VHb) is a type of hemoglobin found in the Gram-negative aerobic bacterium Vitreoscilla that has been shown to contribute to the tolerance of anaerobic stress in multiple plant species. Under the waterlogging condition, transgenic VHb maize seedlings exhibited elevated expression of alcohol dehydrogenase (ADH1) and higher peroxidase (POD) enzyme activity. The two VHb-containing lines, Zheng58 (VHb) and CML50 (VHb), exhibited higher tolerance to waterlogging than their negative control lines (Zheng58 and CML50). Du H *et al*, (2016) has reported that the exogenous VHb (Vitreoscilla hemoglobin) gene confers waterlogging tolerance to the transgenic maize line. In Maize in the place of to the transgenic maize line, the VHb(vitreoscilla hemoglobin) gene is a useful molecular tool for the improvement of waterlogging and submergence-tolerance. Vitreoscilla hemoglobin (VHb) is a type of hemoglobin found in the Gram-negative aerobic bacterium Vitreoscilla that has been shown to contribute to the tolerance of anaerobic stress in multiple plant species. Maize (*Zea mays* L.) is susceptible to waterlogging, causing significant yield loss. In this study, we approached this problem with the introduction of an exogenous VHb gene. Zaidi PH, (2015) has reported that A pair of flanking SNP(single nucleotide polymorphism) markers have been identified for each of the QTL (qualitative trait locus) and high throughput marker assays were developed to facilitate rapid introgression of waterlogging tolerance in tropical maize breeding programs. The most economic option to offset the damage caused by waterlogging is to genetically incorporate tolerance in cultivars that are grown widely in the target agro-ecologies. QTL mapping revealed five QTL on chromosomes 1, 3, 5, 7 and 10, which together explained approximately 30% of phenotypic variance for GY based on evaluation of RIL families under waterlogged conditions, with effects ranging from 520 to 640 kg/ha for individual genomic regions. 13 QTL were identified for various secondary traits associated with waterlogging tolerance, each individually explaining from 3 to 14% of phenotypic variance. Takahashi (2015) has reported that several genes related to cell wall modification and proteolysis are specifically up- or downregulated in cortical cells during lysigenousaerenchyma formation under aerobic conditions with ethylene treatment. The results suggest that ethylene is perceived in stelar cells, cortical cells and outer cell layers in the maize primary root, and that the cortical cell-specific PCD (programmed cell death) is controlled downstream of ethylene perception through subsequent gene expression, which is partly regulated by ROS (reactive oxygen species), in the cortical cells. Internal aeration is important for plants to survive during periods of waterlogging and the ability to form aeraenchyma contributes by creating an aontinuous gas space between the shoots and the roots. Roots of maize (*Zea mays* L.) react to prolonged waterlogging by forming aerenchyma in root cortical cells by programmed cell death (PCB) in response to ethylene. Lu D, (2015) has reported that peak and breakdown viscosities decrease and retro gradation percentage increased when plants were subjected to waterlogging after pollination. In conclusion, waterlogging decreased starch granule size, crystallinity, swelling power, and solubility, resulting in deteriorated starch quality (i.e., low swelling, less sticky and easy to retrograde). Waterlogging frequently occurs in Southern China in summer and significantly affects waxy maize growth. This study investigated the physicochemical properties of starch from six waxy maize varieties exposed to waterlogging for 1-7 days after pollination. Waterlogging decreased the starch granule size. Yu F, (2015), has reported that. The evaluations of five specific physiological parameters (alcohol dehydrogenase activity and GSH (glucocorticoid-Suppressible Hyperaldosteronism), malondialdehyde, adenosine 5 triphosphate and nicotinamide adenine dinucleotide concentrations) were in agreement with the protemomic results. Moreover, bas on the proteomic assay, eight represented genes encoding DAPs (Differential abundant proteins) were selected for validation at the transcribed level. qRT-PCR revealed that the expression levels of these genes correlated with their observe protein abundance. These finding shed light on the complex mechanisms underlying waterlogging tolerance in maize.Wang F, (2015), has reported that The amounts of soil bacteria in C-R and B-R patterns, fungi in B-R rotation pattern, cellulose bacteria in R-R (rape-rice), C-R (corn-rice) and B-R (bean-rice) patterns and N-fixing bacteria in B-R (bean-rice) pattern were improved by 285.7%-403.0%, 221.7%, 64.6-92.2% and 162.2%, respectively. Moreover, the differences in all microorganisms were significant. Thus, based on the experimental results of cold-waterlogged paddy field, it was concluded that changing from single cropping rice system to C-R, R-R and B-R rotation patterns had a good effect in terms of improving total yield and economic benefits, and soil physical and chemical properties were improved. Liu, (2014) has reported that the Yield of maize was increased by 9.5% under RP (ridge tillage with plastic mulch) as compared with RB (ridge tillage without mulch). However, the yield was reduced by 5.0% under FP (flat tillage without mulch), due to the plastic film under flat tillage prevented the infiltration of rainfall and waterlogging occurred. No significant difference in yield was found between RB (ridge tillage without mulch) and FB (flat tillage without mulch). The higher yield of spring maize was limited because of the mismatching in water supply and demand characterized by soil water shortage before the rainy season and abundant soil water storage after the rainy season. Yamauchi *et al.*, (2014) has reported that under well-drained soil, aerenchyma formation is not observed in the root tissue of maize, whereas waterlogged condition induces aerenchyma formation in maize. Aerenchyma formation is attributed to the activity of ethylene in programmed cell death. Waterlogged conditions resulting from episodes of flooding in this region will reoccur as evidence of climate change. Therefore, the need to identify crops from the commonly grown crop species that can tolerate long periods of waterlogging has become foremost. Okra and maize are economically important food crops worldwide. The main objective of the current study was to assess okra and maize plants given exogenous ethylene priming for tolerating long periods of waterlogging. Bai-zhao, (2014) has reported that the leaf chlorophyll content and grain yield of summer maize decreased significantly after waterlogging. The grain yields of DH605 (denghai 605) and ZD958 (zhengan 958) after waterlogging for 6 days at V3 (three leaf stages) were most seriously affected, which were decreased by 32.1% and 35.2%, respectively. Overall, the summer maize was most susceptible to the effect of waterlogging at V3 (3 leaf stage), followed by V6 (six leaf stage) and 10VTtesting stage), and the influence extent increased with the increase of waterlogging duration. Ren, (2014) found that waterlogging for 1 d had little effect on maize production, but waterlogging for more than 3 d resulted in a more than 40% reduction in grain yield; At V6, waterlogging for 5-7 d (as well as 7 d at VT) prevented harvest of summer maize. Previous studies have shown that waterlogging can decrease maize yield. However, results have varied because of the different materials and methods used. Furthermore, most previous studies have been performed with pot experiments. Plants grown in pots have restricted spatial and root growth, which limits the natural responses of plant growth. In addition, few studies have assessed the interaction of waterlogging stage and duration on the ear trait, grain filling, growing periods and dry matter distribution. The objective of this study was to determine the effect of waterlogging for 3 or

6 don yield and growth of field-grown summer maize at the three-leaf stage (V3), six-leaf stage (V6), and the 10th day after the tasseling stage (10VT). Song (2013) has reported that the Due to the improvement of soil water and thermal conditions, the leaf photosynthetic rate (Pr) and transpiration rate (Tr) at jointing stage in jointing stages and without ridging were significantly higher than those in ridge planting, whereas the PS II potential activity (Fv/Fo) and PS II maximal photochemical efficiency (Fv/Fm) had no significant differences among the treatments, indicating that the stomatal factors such as stomata conductivity and stomata limitation were the main factors inducing the photosynthesis differences among the treatments. Furthermore, the Pr (photosynthetic rate) and Tr (transpiration rate) at grain filling stage in ridge planting and jointing stage were higher than those in PP, mainly due to the high water-logging risk in without ridging in strong rainfall season. Consequently, treatment in the jointing stage could promote maize photosynthesis through improving soil water and thermal conditions, and further, increase maize grain yield. Jiang JB,(2013) has reported that the index R800* R550/R680 could be used to quickly extract flooding disaster area by using hyperspectral remote sensing, and would provide information support for disaster relief decisions. The result indicated that the distance of R800 * R550/R680 is more than that of indices' in the early stress stage, illustrated that the index identifiable ability for waterlogging stress is better than other indices, then the index has the strong sensitivity and stability. The objective of the present paper was to study the leaf spectral features of vegetation (maize and beetroot) under waterlogging stress and design a hyperspectral remote sensing model to monitor the flooding disasters through a field simulated experiment. Osman (2013) has reported that expression of most QTL (quantitative trait loci) was influenced by the developmental status. In order to provide additional evidence regarding the role of corresponding genes in waterlogging tolerance, mapping of Expressed Sequence Tags markers and microRNAs were conducted. Seven candidate genes were observed to co-localize with the identified QTL(quantitative trait loci) on chromosomes 1, 4, 6, 7 and 9, and may be important candidate genes for waterlogging tolerance. These results are a good starting point for understanding the genetic basis for selectively expressing of QTL (quantitative trait loci) in different stress periods and the common genetic control mechanism of the co-localized traits. Thirunavukkarasu (2013) has reported that a whole-genome transcriptome assay revealed the specific role of genes in response to waterlogging stress in susceptible and tolerant genotypes. Genes involved in the synthesis of ethylene and auxin, cell wall metabolism, activation of G-proteins and formation of aerenchyma and adventitious roots, were upregulated in the tolerant genotype. Waterlogging causes extensive damage to maize crops in tropical and

subtropical regions. The identification of tolerance genes and their interactions at the molecular level will be helpful to engineer tolerant genotypes. The physical locations of 21 genes expressed in the tolerant genotype were found to correspond with the marker intervals of known QTLs (qualitative trait loci) responsible for the development of adaptive traits. Mano (2013) has reported that A flooding-tolerant genotype, IL#18, was identified; this genotype should be useful for maize breeding. In addition, because the chromosome segments of Z. nicaraguensis in the ILs cover nearly the entire genome and Z. nicaraguensis possesses several unique traits related to flooding tolerance, the ILs should be valuable material for additional QTL(qualitative trait loci) detection and the development of flooding-tolerant maize lines.Nicaraguan teosinte (*Zea nicaraguensis*), a species found in frequently flooded areas, provides useful germplasm for breeding flooding-tolerant maize (Z. mays subsp. mays). The objective of this study was to select flooding-tolerant lines using a library of introgression lines (ILs), each containing a chromosome segment from Z. nicaraguensis in the maize inbred line Mi29. Ahmed (2013) has reported that genetic and environmental interaction, too many genes encoding a trait, and using undesirable populations the mapping of QTL (qualitative trait loci) was hampered to ensure proper growth and yield under waterlogged conditions Steady advances in the field of genomics and proteomics over the years will be helpful to increase the breeding programs which will help to accomplish a significant progress in the field crop variety development and also improvement in near future. Waterlogging response of soybean and major cereal crops, like rice, wheat, barley, and maize and discovery of QTL (qualitative trait loci) related with a tolerance of waterlogging, development of resistant variety. The discovery of comprehensive molecular linkage maps enables us to do the pyramiding of desirable traits to improve in submergence tolerance through MAS(marker-assisted selection). Zhai (2013) has reported that the miRNA targets through degrade sequencing. Many known miRNA targets involving in transcription regulation and reactive oxygen species elimination were found in the degrade libraries, and 17 targets of 10 newly detected miRNAs were identified as well. Moreover, the miRNA-mediated pathways that respond to waterlogging and regulate the induction of crown roots were discussed. This study is a comprehensive survey of responsive miRNAs in waterlogged maize crown roots. The results will help to understand the miRNA expression in response to waterlogging and miRNA-mediated regulation of morphological adaptation to waterlogging in maize. Hernandez-Soriano (2012) has reported that Pb was originally co-precipitated with Al-DOC complexes in the solid phase. The effect of A22 in metal bioavailability, determined as free ion activities (FIA), was mainly controlled by soil moisture regime. For soil 3, metal bioavailability was up to 20 times lower for soil amended with hay, peat or maize compared to soil treated only with A22. The mobility and bioavailability of cadmium, copper, lead, and zinc were evaluated in three soils amended with different organic materials for two moisture regimes. Agricultural and reclamation activities impose fresh inputs of organic matter on the soil while intensive irrigation and rainstorm increase soil waterlogging incidence. Soils added with hay, maize straw or peat at 1% w/w were irrigated, at field capacity (FC) or saturated (S), with an aqueous solution of the anionic surfactant Aerosol 22 (A22), corresponding to an addition of 200 mg/kgsoil/day. Soil solution was extracted after one month and analysed for total soluble metals, dissolved soil organic matter and UV absorbance at 254 nm. Liu Z (2012) has reported that the stress and development related cis-regulatory elements on the promoters of these miRNAs; and a probable miRNA-mediated gene regulatory network in response to short-term waterlogging stress was constructed. The differential expression patterns of miRNAs and their targets in these three inbred lines suggest that the miRNAs are active participants in the signal transduction at the early stage of hypoxia conditions via a gene regulatory network; and crosstalk occurs between different biochemical pathways. Waterlogging of plants leads to low oxygen levels (hypoxia) in the roots and causes a metabolic switch from aerobic respiration to anaerobic fermentation that results in rapid changes in gene transcription and protein synthesis. His research seeks to characterize the microRNA-mediated gene regulatory networks associated with short-term waterlogging. Chugh (2012), has reported that Waterlogging caused strong induction in alcohol dehydrogenase activity in the roots of sensitive and waterlogging tolerant under stress conditions. Aldehyde dehydrogenase activity was significantly increased only in roots of water-tolerant in response to waterlogging. In comparison with sensitive genotype, the tolerant genotype had low H_2O_2 (hydrogen peroxide) and malondialdehyde content in roots under stress conditions. The present studies suggested that tolerant genotype had a greater protective ability due to higher induced activities of antioxidant and ethanolic fermentation systems than sensitive maize genotype. Abiko (2012) has reported that growth of maize was more adversely affected by low oxygen in the root zone (waterlogged soil or stagnant deoxygenated nutrient solution) compared with Z.nicaraguensis. In stagnant deoxygenated solution, Z. nicaraguensis was superior to maize in transporting oxygen from shoot base to root tip due to the formation of larger aerenchyma and a stronger barrier to ROL in adventitious roots. The relationships between the ROL (radial oxygen loss) barrier formation and suberin and lignin depositions in roots. The ROL (radial oxygen loss) barrier, in addition to aerenchyma, would contribute to the waterlogging tolerance of Z. nicaraguensis.Hossain and Uddin, (2011) has reported that the shoot system of plants exhibit certain features, including wilting, premature yellowing of leaves (senescence), stunted plant height, epinasty, stem deformation, shoot length alteration, and leaf area reduction. Furthermore, crops including wheat show sterile floret and reduced grain yield and kernel. Root extension growth in terrestrial plants is arrested because the root tip is intolerant to hypoxic (low oxygen) or anoxic (absence of oxygen) conditions. Prolonged waterlogging will lead to alteration of chemical and physical properties of soil. These soil factors include pH, EC, hydraulic conductance, soil structure, porosity, and organics. Chugh (2011) has reported that the tolerant seedlings had higher GR (glutathione reductase) activity than susceptible genotypes under unstressed conditions. Stress led to decrease in H_2O_2 (hydrogen peroxide) and an increase in glutathione content of both tolerant and susceptible genotypes, but only tolerant genotypes exhibited an increase in ascorbic acid under waterlogging conditions. In the tolerant genotypes, all the enzymes of anaerobic metabolism viz. alcohol dehydrogenase (ADH), aldehyde dehydrogenase (ALDH) and pyruvate decarboxylase (PDC) were upregulated under waterlogging, whereas in susceptible genotypes, only ADH was upregulated, suggesting that efficient upregulation of entire anaerobic metabolic machinery is essential for providing tolerance against waterlogging. The study provides a possible mechanism for waterlogging tolerance in maize. Zou (2011) has reported that the function of the emerging zmP4H family and suggest that AS might have an important role in the regulation of the expression profile of this gene family under waterlogging stress. In animals, prolyl 4-hydroxylases (P4Hs) are regarded as oxygen sensors under hypoxia stress, but little is known about their role in the response to waterlogging in maize. A comprehensive genome-wide analysis of P4H genes of maize (zmP4H genes) was carried out, including gene structures, phylogeny, protein motifs, chromosomal locations and expression patterns under waterlogging. The diverse transcripts generated from AS were expressed at different levels, suggesting that zmP4H genes were under specific control by post-transcriptional regulation under waterlogging stress in the line HZ32. Wang (2011) has reported that the phylogenetic relationships of Zea species inferred from the ITS sequences are highly concordant with the RAPD evidence that resolved two major subgenus clades. Both RAPD and ITS sequence analyses indicate that *Zea nicaraguensis* is more closely related to Zea luxurians than the other teosintes and cultivated maize, which should be regarded as a section Luxuriantes species. Genetic relationship of a newly discovered teosinte from Nicaragua, Zea nicaraguensis with waterlogging tolerance, was determined based on randomly amplified polymorphic DNA (RAPD) markers and the internal transcribed spacer (ITS) sequences of nuclear ribosomal DNA using 14 accessions from Zea species. RAPD analysis showed that a total of 5,303 fragments were produced by 136 random decamer primers, of which 84.86% bands were polymorphic. Yamauchi (2011) has reported that respiratory burst oxidase homolog (RBOH) gene encodes a homolog of gp91 (phox) in NADPH oxidase, and has a role in the generation of reactive oxygen species (ROS). Recently, we found that, during aerenchyma formation, RBOH was up-regulated in all maize root tissues examined, whereas an ROS scavenging-related metallothionein (MT) gene was down-regulated specifically in cortical cells. Together, these changes should lead to high accumulations of ROS in the root cortex, thereby inducing PCD for aerenchyma formation. As further evidence of the involvement of ROS in root aerenchyma formation, the PCD was inhibited by diphenyleneiodonium (DPI), an NADPH oxidase inhibitor. Based on these results, we propose a model of cortical cell-specific PCD for root aerenchyma formation. o adapt to waterlogging, maize (*Zea mays*) forms lysigenousaerenchyma in root cortex as a result of ethylene-promoted programmed cell death (PCD). Rajhi (2011), has reported that the differentially expressed genes included genes related to the generation or scavenging of reactive oxygen species, Ca^{2+} signaling, and cell wall loosening and degradation. The results of this study should lead to a better understanding of the mechanism of root lysigenousaerenchyma formation. To adapt to waterlogging in soil, some gramineous plants, such as maize (*Zea mays*), form lysigenousaerenchyma in the root cortex. Ethylene, which is accumulated during waterlogging, promotes aerenchyma formation. However, the molecular mechanism of aerenchyma formation is not understood. The aim of this study was to identify aerenchyma formation-associated genes expressed in maize roots as a basis for understanding the molecular mechanism of aerenchyma formation. Steffen (2010), induction of alcohol dehydrogenase with resulting increased plant survival relies on the balanced activities of a small Rop G protein and its deactivating protein RopGAP4. Identifying the general mechanisms of G protein signaling in hypoxia adaptation of plants is one of the tasks ahead.

Waterlogging or flooding are frequently or constitutively encountered by many plant species. The resulting reduction in endogenous O_2 concentration poses a severe threat. Numerous adaptations at the anatomical, morphological and metabolic level help plants to either escape low oxygen conditions or to endure them. Formation of aerenchyma or rapid shoot elongation are escape responses, as is the formation of adventitious roots. The metabolic shift from aerobic respiration to anaerobic fermentation contributes to a basal energy supply at low oxygen conditions. Ethylene plays a central role in hypoxic stress signaling, and G proteins have been recognized as crucial signal transducers in various hypoxic signaling pathways. Zau (2010) has reported that the late response to waterlogging in maize roots involves a broad spectrum of genes, which are mainly associated with two response processes: defense at the early stage and adaption at the late stage. Signal transduction plays a key role in activating genes related to the tolerance mechanism for survival during prolonged waterlogging. The crosstalk between carbon and amino acid metabolism reveals that amino acid metabolism performs two main roles at the late stage: the regulation of cytoplasmic pH and energy supply through the breakdown of the carbon skeleton.. In this study, the transcriptome at the late stage of waterlogging was assayed in root cells of the tolerant inbred line HZ32, using suppression subtractive hybridization (SSH). Zang (2010) has reported that GUS(staining for β-glucuronidase) expression was not observed in the roots and leaves of Hz32 zmzf transgenic lines, even under submerged conditions, indicating that the Hz32 zmzf promoter was non-functional because of the deletion of three AREs (anaerobic response elements). We propose that the Mo17 zmzf (transgenic lines) promoter was inducible by waterlogging, highly active, and root-specific, and might be useful for the genetic engineering of waterlogging tolerance. Jiru (2010) has reported that surge and deficit irrigation technologies not only improve water productivity but also enhance environmental sustainability. Results have shown that surge and deficit irrigation practices increase water productivity by 62% and 58%, respectively, when compared to traditional management.

CONCLUSION

The study also found out that these practices reduce the adverse environmental impacts (waterlogging and salinity) of traditional management by minimizing deep percolation and tail water losses. Total irrigation depth was reduced by 12% (for surge) and 27% (for deficit) when compared to traditional management. Therefore, exploring environmentally friendly water-saving irrigation strategies is essential for achieving food and environmental security. In northern Ethiopia, where traditional furrow irrigation is widely practiced, water mismanagement and its undesirable environmental impact are rampant.

REFERENCES

Du H, Zhu J, Su H, Huang M, Wang H, Ding S, Zhang B, Luo A, Wei S, Tian X. and Xu, Y. (2017). Bulked Segregant RNA-seq Reveals Differential Expression and SNPs of Candidate Genes Associated with Waterlogging Tolerance in Maize. *Frontiers in Plant Science*, 8, 1022.

Huang M, Wang H, Ding S, Zhang B, Luo A, Wei S, Tian X. and Xu, Y. (2017). Bulked Segregant RNA-seq Reveals Differential Expression and SNPs of Candidate Genes Associated with Waterlogging Tolerance in Maize. *Frontiers in Plant Science*, 8, 1022.

Khaldun ABM, Zonayed-Ull-Noor MMA, Hoque MAM and Rohman MM. (2010). Evaluation of Waterlogged Tolerant Maize (Zea mays L.) Hybrids in Bangladesh.

Liang K, Zhang Z, Du D, Zhang X, Zhao H, Basir UI. and Qiu F. (2018). Dissecting the Genetic Architecture of Waterlogging Stress-related Traits Uncovers a Key Waterlogging Tolerance Gene in Maize. *Theoretical and Applied Genetics*, 131(11), 2299-2310.

Maestrini B. and Basso B. (2018). Drivers of within-field Spatial and Temporal Variability of Crop yield Across the US Midwest. *Scientific Reports*, 8(1), 14833.

Panozzo A, Dal Cortivo C, Ferrari M, Vicelli B, Varotto S., and Vamerali T, (2019). Morphological Changes and Expressions of AOX1A, CYP81D8 and Putative PFP Genes in a Large Set of Commercial Maize Hybrids under Extreme Waterlogging. *Frontiers in Plant Science*, 10, 62.

Rafique S, (2019). Differential Expression of Leaf Proteome of Tolerant and Susceptible Maize (*Zea mays* L.) Genotype in Response to Multiple Abiotic Stresses. *Biochemistry and Cell Biology*.

Ren B, Dong S, Zhao B, Liu P. and Zhang J (2017). Responses of Nitrogen Metabolism, uptake and Translocation of Maize to Waterlogging at Different Growth Stages. *Frontiers in Plant Science*, 8, 1216.

Salah A, Zhan M, Cao C, Han Y, Ling L, Liu Z, Li P, Ye M and Jiang, Y (2019). γ-Aminobutyric Acid Promotes Chloroplast Ultrastructure, Antioxidant Capacity, and Growth of Waterlogged Maize Seedlings. *Scientific Reports*, 9(1), 484.

Wang F, Wang MJ, Su SH, Wang YY, Su YH, Meng GX, Sun Y, Qi H. and Jiang Y. (2018). Effects of Straw Returning on Maize yield and Root System Spatial Distribution under Water Stress. *Ying yong sheng taixuebao. The Journal of Applied Ecology*, 29(11), 3643-3648.

Vwioko E, Adinkwu O., and El-Esawi MA. (2017). Comparative Physiological, Biochemical, and Genetic Responses to Prolonged Waterlogging Stress in Okra and Maize given Exogenous Ethylene Priming. *Frontiers in Physiology*, 8, 632.

Watanabe K, Takahashi H, Sato S, Nishiuchi S, Omori F, Malik AI, Colmer TD, Mano Y. and Nakazono M. (2017). A Major Locus Involved in the Formation of the Radial Oxygen Loss Barrier in Adventitious Roots of Teosinte Zeanicaraguensis is Located on the Short Arm of Chromosome 3. *Plant, Cell & Environment*, 40(2), 304-316.

Zhang L, Wu W, Wang S, Chen H, Song Y, Peng C, Jing L. and Li J. (2018). Optimal Nitrogen Regimes Compensate for the Impacts of Seedlings Subjected to Waterlogging Stress in Summer Maize. *PloS one*, 13(10), 0206210.

Pages: 55-73

Irrigation Practices and Sustainable Agriculture
Edited by: **Dr. Prasann Kumar and Dr. Pawan Kumar 'Bharti'**
ISBN: 978-93-88854-31-3
Edition: **2020**
Published by: **Discovery Publishing House Pvt. Ltd., New Delhi (India)**

4 Evaluation of Organic Nutrient-Management Practices in Rice–Tomato–Okra System under Irrigated Conditions

[1]Alok Kumar Patra, [2]L.M. Garnayak and [3]K.N. Mishra

ABSTRACT

A long-term field trial on organic nutrient management in rice (Oryza sativa L.)–(Solanum lycopersicum L.)–okra (Abelmoschus esculentus L.) cropping system was conducted continuously for eight years from 2005-06 to 2012-13 in the Hirakud command area of western Odisha in a sandy loam soil with 5.9 pH and 7.6 g/kg organic carbon at Chiplima. Eight treatments comprising of five organic, two integrated and one inorganic approach of nutrient management were tested under irrigated condition. The individual crop yields and rice equivalent yield (REY) of the system during the first crop cycle were highest with the inorganic treatment closely followed by the integrated approach of 50% recommended dose of fertilizers (RDF) + 50% of N as farm yard manure (FYM). Organic treatments reduced the system yield by 5.5 to 8.4% and RDF + recycling of crop residues by 4.9% over the inorganic treatment in the first year. After first three crop cycles (conversion period), the mean system yield with organic treatment comprising of supply of 1/3rd N each through FYM, green manuring of dhaincha (Sesbania aculeata) or vermicompost and neem cake + Azospirillum or Azotobacter + phosphate solubilizing bacteria (PSB) was equivalent to that of inorganic and integrated approach. However, the other organic approaches without biofertilizers were low yielder than inorganic treatment. After conversion period (4th to 8th crop cycles) all the organic and integrated treatments except one with 50% N as FYM + biofertilizers + rock phosphate (RP) increased

[1] Professor (Agronomy), All India Coordinated Research Project on Integrated Farming Systems, Odisha University of Agriculture and Technology, Bhubaneswar - 751 003 (Odisha) (India)
[2] Professor (Agronomy), College of Agriculture, Odisha University of Agriculture and Technology, Bhubaneswar - 751 003 (Odisha) (India)
[3] Professor (Soil Science), College of Agriculture, Odisha University of Agriculture and Technology, Bhubaneswar - 751 003 (Odisha) (India)

system yield over the inorganic treatment and the increment was the highest (12%) in the organic treatment comprising of FYM + green manuring or vermicompost + neem oil cake + Azospirillum or Azotobacter + PSB. The nutrient uptake was the maximum in inorganic and integrated treatment in the first year and in organic and integrated treatment after the conversion period. The organic nutrient management package increased the soil organic carbon (SOC) and available N, P and K at the end of 8th crop cycle over the initial and the build-up was maximum in the soil applied with 33.3% N each through FYM, dhaincha and neem cake + Azospirillum/Azotobacter + PSB. But inorganic treatment exhibited a negative balance. The microbial population in terms of colony forming units (cfu) increased in a higher rate in soils with organic nutrient supply system (bacteria 32.4 to 37.1%, fungi 30.2 to 34.4% and actinomycetes 29.3 to 35.9%) compared to the inorganic source of nutrient supply system (bacteria 11.2%, fungi 5.5 % and actinomycetes 11.3%) after 8th cropping system cycle over initial status. The microbial biomass carbon (MBC) of the soils with organic sources of nutrient supply was enhanced considerably (53.4% to 61.8%) over the initial level (104.7 to 118.2 ìg C/ g). The MBC/SOC ratio in soils under organic nutrient management practices was much higher (1.83 to 2.07%) than inorganic treatment suggesting higher substrate availability through build-up of organic matter in soils due to organic approach of nutrient management in high value cropping system.

Keywords: *Cropping system, Microbial biomass carbon, Organic sources of nutrient supply, Soil microbial population, Sustainable yield index, System yield.*

INTRODUCTION

Rice (*Oryza sativa* L.)–rice is the predominant cropping system in the Hirakud command area of western Odisha. Cropping systems involving cereal after cereal for years had led to mining of nutrients from the soil that resulted in deterioration of soil health (John *et al.*, 2001; Porpavai *et al.*, 2011). Continuous rice–rice cropping system results in rapid decline in soil fertility and thus requires a special attention. Inclusion of vegetables in the cropping system was more beneficial than cereal after cereal (Kumpawat, 2001; Sharma *et al.*, 2007). A few farmers prefer vegetables during *rabi* and summer seasons in canal tail-ends where summer rice could experience water scarcity towards the late growth period. Thus, crop diversification during *rabi* and summer seasons plays a significant role in augmenting the farm income per unit area by integrating small duration high value crops with high water and nutrient use efficiency (Sharma *et al.*, 2004; Gangwar and Ram, 2005; Pramanik and Ravisankar, 2007). Several intensive rice based cropping systems have been identified for the region through the experiments conducted at Chiplima by the All India Coordinated Research Project on Integrated Farming Systems. Rice–tomato (*Solanum lycopersicum* L.)–okra (*Abelmoschus esculentus* L.) has been identified as the most productive and profitable cropping system for the command area.

Cropping systems involving high value vegetable crops remove considerable quantum of nutrients from the soil. Per tonne of economic produce, rice crop removes about 20.1 kg N, 11.2 kg P and 30.0 kg K; tomato removes 2.8 kg N, 0.6 kg P and 3.8 kg K and okra crop removes 3.0 kg N, 1.3 kg P and 4.5 kg K, besides appreciable quantity of secondary and micro-nutrients (Tiwari, 2001). Thus, promotion of organic farming is being viewed as farming practice with distinct advantages of sustainability of crop production. Though positive role of organic residues, including green manures on soils and crops has been well documented (Patnaik and Rao, 1979; Rupela *et al.*, 2006), information on organic package for location specific cropping system is very meager to understand the role of organic farming on soil health, production, profitability and sustainability. It is a common belief that yields of several crops are reduced during the initial years under organic farming, but many experiments were conducted only for three or four years consecutively and often only with a specific crop; rather than in a well defined high productivity cropping system (Dubey *et al.*, 2014; Rao *et al.*, 2014).

Keeping the above facts in mind, an experiment was designed on rice–tomato–okra system with various organic and integrated nutrient management practices for consecutive eight years to study and compare the overall productivity of the system with that of the inorganic nutrient management practice and to find out the impact of various nutrient management practices on soil properties.

MATERIALS AND METHODS

The experiment was conducted consecutively for eight years from 2005-06 to 2012-13 in a fixed plot trial under Hirakud command at Regional Research and Technology Transfer Station, Odisha University of Agriculture and Technology, Chiplima, Odisha (21° 38′ N, 83° 90′ E, 144 m above MSL). The Hirakud command area comes under West Central Table Land agro-climatic zone of the state. The sedentary soils of this tract are of Red and mixed Red and Yellow Genetic class. It has a hot humid climate with mean annual rainfall of 1496 mm. The mean maximum and minimum temperature were 33.8 and 22.0° C, respectively. The soils are deep sandy loam in surface with 62% sand, 18% silt and 20% clay and belong to *Typic Haplustalfs* as sub-group levels. The soil of the experimental site was sandy loam, having *p*H 5.9; organic carbon 7.6 g/kg, available N, P and K of 294.2, 10.1 and 121.4 kg/ha, respectively. The experiment was laid out in randomized block design with eight treatments as detailed in table 4.1 and replicated thrice.

Table 4.1: Treatment details

Treatment	*Kharif* (Rice)	*Rabi* (Tomato)	Summer (Okra)
T_1	50% N as RDF + 50% N as FYM (8 t/ha)	50% RDF + 50% N as FYM (10 t/ha)	50% RDF + 50% N as FYM (8 t/ha)
T_2	Different organic sources equivalent to 1/3 of recommended N (1/3 N as FYM @ 5.5 t/ha, 1/3N as *dhaincha*, 1/3 N as neem (*Azadirachta indica*) oilcake)	Different organic sources equivalent to 1/3 of recommended N(1/3 N as FYM @ 6.7 t/ha, 1/3N as vermicompost, 1/3 N as neem oilcake)	Different organic sources equivalent to 1/3 of recommended N(1/3 N as FYM @ 5.5 t/ha, 1/3N as vermicompost, 1/3 N as neem oilcake)
T_3	Same as T_2	Same as T_2	T_2+ cowpea (*Vigna sinensis*) as a trap crop (1:1) in additive series
T_4	T_2 + manual weed control + biopesticides (neem oil and pot manure*)	T_2 + manual weed control + biopesticides (neem oil and pot manure*)	T_2 + manual weed control + biopesticides (neem oil and pot manure*)
T_5	50% N as FYM + *Azospirillum* + RP + PSB (soil application)	50% N as FYM + *Azotobacter* + RP + PSB (soil application)	50% N as FYM + *Azotobacter* + RP + PSB (soil application)
T_6,	T_2 +*Azospirillum* + PSB	T_2 +*Azotobacter* + PSB	T_2 + *Azotobacter*+ PSB
T_7	100% NPK + $ZnSO_4$ @ 25 kg/ha	100% NPK + gypsum @ 110 kg/ha + borax @ 10 kg/ha + ammonium molybdate @ 0.8 kg/ha	100% NPK + gypsum @ 110 kg/ha + borax @ 10 kg/ha + ammonium molybdate @ 0.8 kg/ha
T_8	T_7 + crop residue recycling**	T_7 + crop residue recycling**	T_7 + crop residue recycling**

RDF, recommended dose of fertilizers; FYM, farm yard manure; RP, rock phosphate; PSB, phosphate solubulizing bacteria

RDF (in kg N-P-K kg/ha): rice, 80-17.5-33; tomato, 100-33-33; okra, 80-17.5-33

*Pot manure or *handi khata* as locally called is prepared with karanja leaves (*Pongamia pinnata*) 0.5 kg, bel (*Aegle marmelos*) leaves 0.5 kg, *arakha* leaves (*Calotropis* sp.) 1 kg, neem (*Azadirachta indica*) leaves 1 kg, jaggery 0.2 kg, cow urine 2 liters and fresh cow dung 1 kg. All the materials and chopped leaves are kept inside an earthen pot and thoroughly mixed. Then the mouth of pot is covered and kept under shade. After a week, another 2 liters of cow urine is poured inside the pot. In 3 weeks, the manure is ready to use in crop fields. The liquid extract is diluted with water and sprayed on the plants.

**After harvest the total quantity of plant residues were okra plant residue 4.2 t/ha were available for recycling. Average nutrient content, rice straw N 0.43, P 0.24, K 1.33%, tomato haulm N 1.76, P 0.09, K 1.09% and okra plant residue N 1.89, P 0.38, K 2.09%

The organic sources used in the experiments are FYM (N, P, K: 0.58%, 0.29%, 0.66%), vermicompost (N, P, K: 1.67%, 1.04%, 1.59%), neem cake (N, P, K: 4.38%, 0.89%, 1.35%), green manuring of *dhaincha* (*Sesbania aculeata*) (N, P, K: 2.86%, 0.59%, 1.21%) and biofertilizers such as *Azotobacter, Azospirillum* and phosphate solubilizing bacteria (PSB). The inorganic sources are N, P and K containing fertilizers such as urea (46% N), single super phosphate (16% P_2O_5) and muriate of potash (60% K_2O), respectively, zinc sulphate (21% Zn), gypsum (21% Ca, 17% S), borax (10% B) and ammonium molybdate (52% Mo). Initial soil samples (during 2005) and soil samples at the end of each cropping cycle (up to 8th cropping cycle) drawn from a depth of 0-15 cm from individual plots were processed in the laboratory and analyzed for SOC (Walkley and Black, 1934), available N (Subbiah and Asija, 1956), P (Olsen *et al.*, 1954) and K (Knudsen *et al.*, 1982). A portion of fresh soil samples were passed through a 2 mm sieve and stored at 4°C for determination of microbial population (Dhingra and Sinclair, 1993) and MBC (Vance *et al.*, 1987). The MBC was estimated from the equation, MBC = 2.64 Ec, where Ec is the difference between organic carbon extracted from the K_2SO_4 extract of fumigated and non-fumigated soils.

In case of organic nutrient management, all manures were applied before final land preparation for transplanting of rice and at planting of tomato and okra in pits/furrows. In case of inorganic nutrient management, full quantity of P and K were applied as basal in all the crops and N was applied in split doses. In rice, 25% of N was applied as basal, 50% of N was top dressed at tillering and rest 25% of N at panicle initiation stages. In tomato and okra 50% of N was applied as basal and rest N was applied in two equal split doses at 25 and 45 days after planting. The crops were irrigated as per the requirements. Standard agronomic management practices were followed for each crop. The experimental details are presented in table 4.2.

Table 4.2: Experimental details

Design		Randomized block design
Crop sequence		Rice–tomato–okra
Variety	Rice	Khandagiri
	Tomato	Utkal Kumari
	Okra	Arka Anamika
Gross plot size		20 m × 15 m
Net plot size	Rice	18.8 m × 14 m
	Tomato	18.5 m × 14 m
	Okra	19.0 m × 14 m
Date of sowing	Rice (nursery)	Last week of June
	Tomato (nursery)	1st week of November
	Okra	3rd week of March

(Table Contd...)

Design		Randomized block design
Date of transplanting	Rice	3rd week of July
	Tomato	1st week of December
Date of harvesting	Rice	3rd week of October
	Tomato	1st week of March (final plucking)
	Okra	3rd week of June (final plucking)

Crop yields were recorded at the end of each season and rice equivalent yield (REY) was computed at the end of each cropping cycle as per the formula given below. System yield was obtained by adding REY of component crops.

REY (of crop X) = $Y \times (P_x/P_y)$

Y= yield of tomato/okra in each year

P_x = price of tomato/okra during 8th crop cycle, i.e., 2012-13

P_y = price of rice during 8th crop cycle, i.e., 2012-13

The first three crop cycles were taken as 'conversion period' and the next five years' yields were taken as 'after conversion period' and the mean yields of 'conversion period' and 'after conversion period' were calculated. Overall mean yield was also calculated taking yields of all the eight years. The treatment with recommended dose of inorganic nutrients i.e., T_7 was taken as reference treatment and increase or decrease in system yield was calculated for the 'conversion period', 'after conversion period' and 'overall mean' over this treatment for comparison.

Economic efficiency in terms of /ha/day was worked out by net returns of the system divided by 365 days. For economic analysis (cost of cultivation and gross return) cost of inputs and price of outputs were used from eighth cycle (2012-13) for all the years. Sustainable yield index (SYI) for each treatment was also calculated (Singh *et al.*, 1990) and the 'best fit polynomial equation' was developed for the treatment. Statistical analyses were carried out using standard methodology of randomized block design.

RESULTS AND DISCUSSION

Crop yields and System yield

The individual crop yields and system yield in terms of rice equivalent yield (REY) in the first crop cycle were highest with T_1, i.e., 50% of the RDF + 50% of N as FYM, which was closely followed by T_7, i.e., the recommended dose of fertilizers (RDF) including secondary and micro nutrients (zinc sulphate to rice, gypsum, borax and ammonium molybdate to tomato and okra) (Table 4.3). Application of 50% N as FYM + *Azospirillum* + RP + PSB (T_5) recorded the the lowest yield during the first year and the reduction in system yield was as high as 12.7% as compared to T_7 (Table 4.4).

Table 4.3: Effect of nutrient management packages on crop yield (t/ha) in rice–tomato–okra system in different phases of crop cycles at Chiplima

Treatment	Initial yield level (1st year)				Mean yield of 'conversion period' (1st-3rd cropping system cycles)				Mean yield of 'after conversion period' (4th-8th cropping system cycles)				Overall mean yield (1st-8th cropping system cycles)			
	Kharif	*Rabi*	Summer	REY	*Kharif*	*Rabi*	Summer	REY	*Kharif*	*Rabi*	Summer	REY	*Kharif*	*Rabi*	Summer	REY
T_1,	5.61	13.88	4.80	20.07	5.20	13.91	5.37	20.20	4.45	15.69	6.08	21.39	4.73	15.02	5.82	20.95
T_2,	4.85	12.30	5.00	18.35	5.06	13.10	5.32	19.43	4.34	15.78	5.60	20.91	4.61	14.78	5.50	20.36
T_3,	4.99	12.52	4.88	18.52	5.37	13.23	5.11	19.64	4.60	16.06	5.63	21.40	4.89	15.00	5.44	20.74
T_4,	4.78	12.44	5.05	18.42	4.80	13.33	5.28	19.29	4.47	16.01	5.62	21.22	4.59	15.00	5.49	20.50
T_5,	4.79	11.75	4.55	17.48	4.71	12.72	4.77	18.30	4.18	14.76	5.34	19.76	4.38	14.00	5.12	19.21
T_6,	4.80	13.08	5.05	18.90	5.14	13.50	5.47	19.93	4.68	16.90	6.76	23.11	4.85	15.62	6.28	21.92
T_7,	5.82	13.30	4.96	20.01	5.10	13.54	5.26	19.73	4.17	15.56	5.69	20.66	4.52	14.80	5.53	20.31
T_8,	5.43	13.27	4.35	19.03	5.20	13.48	5.16	19.69	4.31	15.52	5.71	20.79	4.64	14.76	5.50	20.37
SEm ±	0.16	0.26	0.10	0.33	0.08	0.13	0.08	0.22	0.07	0.23	0.16	0.36	0.06	0.17	0.13	0.29
CD (P=0.05)	0.47	0.76	0.30	0.98	0.24	0.38	0.24	0.65	0.21	0.68	0.47	1.06	0.19	0.50	0.39	0.85

Table 4.4: Percent increase/decrease in system yield in different phases of investigation in rice–tomato–okra system under various nutrient management packages compared to recommended fertilizers at Chiplima

Treatment	Initial yield level (%)	Mean yield increase/decrease up to conversion period (%) (1st-3rd crop cycles)	Mean yield increase/decrease after conversion period (%) (4th-8th crop cycles)	Overall mean yield increase/decrease (%) (1st-8th crop cycles)
T_1	0.3	2.4	3.5	3.1
T_2	–8.3	–1.5	1.2	0.2
T_3	–7.4	–0.5	3.6	2.1
T_4	–7.9	–2.2	2.7	0.9
T_5	–12.7	–7.2	–4.3	–5.4
T_6	–5.5	1.0	11.9	7.9
T_7	0.0	0.0	0.0	0.0
T_8	–4.9	–0.2	0.6	0.3

Organic treatments T_2, T_3, T_4 and T_6 reduced the system yields by about 8.3, 7.4 7.9 and 5.5 %, respectively. Even supplementing the RDF with crop residue recycling (T_8) could not improve the yield of the crops; rather it reduced the system yield by 4.9% over the T_7 (Table 4.4). Dubey *et al.* (2014) got the similar results in rice–potato–okra system after four years of experimentation at Jabalpur. After four years of experiments in *kharif* rice at Maruteru in Andhra Pradesh Rao *et al.* (2014) also concluded that though organic farming had an edge over inorganic farming to sustain the soil health and grain quality, but this practice was less productive as compared to inorganic or integrated nutrient management practices.

Reduction in yields due to replacement of chemical fertilizers with organics decreased during the 'conversion period'. After first three crop cycles, the mean system yield with organic treatment T_6 (FYM + green manuring or vermin–compost + neem cake + *Azospirillum/Azotobacter* + PSB) was almost the same as that of inorganic treatment (T_7). Integrated approach of 50% RDF + 50% of N as FYM (T_1) increased the mean system yield by 2.4% over the inorganic treatment (T_7); however, the other organic treatments without RP and biofertilizers (T_2, T_3 and T_4) were low yielder than the T_7. The reduction in mean system yield in T_5 was as high as 7.2 % in comparison to T_7 (Table 4.4).

During the 'after conversion period' (4th to 8th crop cycles) all the treatments except T_5 (50% N as FYM + *Azospirillum/Azotobacter* + RP + PSB) increased the individual mean crop yields and mean system yields over the inorganic treatment (T_7) (Table 4.3). The increase in mean system yield of 4th to 8th crop cycles in T_6 was as high as 11.9% over T_7 (Table 4.4). The trend was also same for the overall mean yield (1st to 8th crop cycle).

SUSTAINABLE YIELD INDEX

Application of 1/3rd N each through FYM, green manuring of dhaincha and neem oilcake + *Azospirillum* + PSB to rice followed by FYM + vermicompost + neem oilcake + *Azotobacter* + PSB to both tomato and okra recorded highest sustainable yield index of 0.83. Application of 50% N as FYM + *Azospirillum* + RP + PSB to rice and 50% N as FYM + *Azotobacter* + RP + PSB to both tomato and okra recorded lowest sustainable yield index of 0.75 (Table 4.5).

SYSTEM ECONOMICS

Application of 1/3rd N each through FYM, green manuring of *dhaincha* and neem oilcake + *Azospirillum* + PSB to rice followed by FYM + vermicompost + neem oilcake + *Azotobacter* + PSB to both tomato and okra recorded highest mean (1st to 8th cropping system cycles) gross return 2,59,483/ha (Table 4.6). However, highest system net return 1,00,679 with highest benefit: cost ratio 1.79 and economic efficiency 276/ha/day was realized with application of 100% NPK + $ZnSO_4$ @ 25 kg/ha to rice and 100% NPK + gypsum @ 110 kg/ha + borax @ 10 kg/ha + ammonium molybdate @ 0.8 kg/ha to tomato and okra. This was due to higher cost of cultivation in case of organic treatment which also include transportation cost of huge quantity of organic manure. Organic treatment incurred about 35,000/ha more cost than the inorganic treatment which restricted the net return/ha.

Table 4.5: Yield trend equations for system yield in rice–tomato–okra system during 8 years of investigation (best fit polynomial equation)

Treatment	System yield	R^2	SYI
T1	$y = -0.075x^2 + 0.851x + 19.03$	0.141	0.82
T2	$y = -0.113x^2 + 1.338x + 17.23$	0.628	0.81
T3	$y = -0.133x^2 + 1.572x + 17.06$	0.709	0.82
T4	$y = -0.113x^2 + 1.416x + 17.01$	0.565	0.80
T5	$y = -0.139x^2 + 1.518x + 15.93$	0.378	0.75
T6	$y = -0.230x^2 + 2.726x + 15.52$	0.711	0.83
T7	$y = -0.098x^2 + 1.009x + 18.28$	0.219	0.81
T8	$y = -0.134x^2 + 1.427x + 17.37$	0.347	0.80

NUTRIENT UPTAKE

The pattern of total nutrient uptake (Table 4.7) almost followed the trend of the system yield (Table 4.3) as nutrient uptake is the function of yield and nutrient concentration out of which yield is the main deciding factor (Meena *et al.*, 2011). In the first year (2005-06), the maximum uptake of 302.9 kg N, 60.7 kg P and 490.4 kg K/ha was obtained in the integrated nutrient management treatment (T_1) closely followed by inorganic treatment (T_7) with corresponding values of 302.6, 61.6 and 486.5 kg/ha (Table 4.6). On the other hand, the crops under organic treatment involving FYM + green manuring or vermi–compost + neem cake + *Azospirillum/Azotobacter* + PSB (T_6) removed the maximum of 342.3 kg N, 71.5 kg P and 568.7 kg K/ha followed by the INM practice of 50% RDF + 50% N as FYM (T_1), when averaged over the eight crop cycles. On an average, the organic treatment (T_6) removed 28.2, 10.3 and 46.5 kg more N, P and K/ha, respectively than the inorganic treatment (T_7) at the end of 8th crop cycle (Table 4.6). The increase in nutrient uptake by the cropping system at end of the 8th crop cycle over first crop cycle was also the maximum of 14.4, 12.6 and 19.6 per cent for N, P and K, respectively in the organic treatment (T_6). Higher availability of nutrients under organic sources might have improved the physiological and metabolic activities in crops leading to higher biomass production and higher uptake (Shalini Pilai *et al.*, 2007).

Table 4.6: Economics of rice–tomato–okra cropping system

Treatment	8th cropping system cycle					Mean of 1st to 8th cropping system cycles				
	Gross return (×10³ /ha)	Total cost (×10³ /ha)	Net return (×10³ /ha)	Economic efficiency (/ha/day)	Benefit: cost ratio	Gross return (×10³ /ha)	Total cost (×10³ /ha)	Net return (×10³ /ha)	Economic efficiency	Benefit: cost ratio (/ha/day)
T_1	245.0	134.8	110.2	302	1.82	229.9	134.8	95.1	261	1.71
T_2	224.9	158.8	66.2	181	1.42	225.1	158.8	66.4	182	1.42
T_3	231.9	158.8	73.1	200	1.46	230.4	158.8	71.6	196	1.45
T_4	244.5	161.8	82.8	227	1.51	237.3	161.8	75.5	207	1.47
T_5	239.6	130.7	108.9	298	1.83	231.5	130.7	100.8	276	1.77
T_6	254.9	162.0	92.9	255	1.57	259.5	162.0	97.5	267	1.60
T_7	238.3	127.1	111.2	305	1.88	227.8	127.1	100.7	276	1.79
T_8	217.8	131.6	86.3	236	1.66	212.0	131.6	80.4	220	1.61

Sale Price (/t): rice grain, 11000; rice straw, 1000; tomato, 8000; okra, 10000

Table 4.7: Changes in nutrient uptake under various nutrient management packages in rice–tomato–okra system at Chiplima

Treatment	Initial nutrient uptake (kg/ha), at end of 1st crop cycle			Average uptake (kg/ha), from first crop cycle to last crop cycle			% changes over initial (last year vs. first year)			Changes over T_7 average		
	N	P	K	N	P	K	N	P	K	N	P	K
T_1	302.9	60.7	490.4	319.8	62.6	526.0	5.03	4.54	12.14	5.5	1.4	3.8
T_2	279.2	55.7	464.0	304.0	57.7	511.9	9.48	6.75	15.91	–10.3	–3.5	–10.3
T_3	283.0	60.2	467.0	311.4	63.8	522.8	9.69	7.33	16.80	–2.9	2.6	0.6
T_4	286.2	58.7	467.5	314.4	61.3	521.6	11.20	7.89	17.73	0.1	0.1	–0.6
T_5	266.7	53.2	444.8	292.3	55.9	494.3	7.98	4.72	14.17	–22.0	–5.3	–27.9
T_6	282.1	56.3	475.8	342.5	71.5	568.7	14.39	12.55	19.55	28.2	10.3	46.5
T_7	302.6	61.1	486.5	314.3	61.2	522.2	–0.54	–1.65	8.47	0.0	0.0	0.0
T_8	284.9	56.4	470.0	308.2	58.6	516.1	7.49	5.58	14.98	–6.1	–2.6	–6.1
SEm ±	4.53	1.06	5.35	5.24	1.42	6.10	5.45	1.81	7.96			
CD (P=0.05)	13.51	3.17	16.02	15.62	4.25	18.12	10.80	5.40	23.72			

SOIL ORGANIC CARBON

Soil organic matter (SOM) is an important determinant of soil fertility, productivity and sustainability and the dynamics of SOM are influenced by agricultural management practices such as tillage, mulching, removal of crop residues and application of organic and mineral fertilizers (Ngwira *et al.*, 2012). The initial status of soil organic carbon (SOC) of the experimental site was medium to high (7.40 to 7.93 g/kg). Addition of organics over the years resulted in dramatic changes in the SOC contents (Table 4.8 and 4.9) of treatments T_2 to T_6 at the end of the 8th cropping cycle and the increase was in the tune of 17.9 to 22.8% over the initial. The elevation of SOC was maximum in the soil added with 33.3%N each through FYM, *dhaincha* and neem cake + *Azospirillum* + PSB to rice followed by similar combination with FYM, vermi–compost, neem cake + *Azotobacter* + PSB to both tomato and okra (T_6). Continuous addition of inorganic fertilizers, however registered a negative balance (–10.9%) in SOC over the initial status. The higher buildup of SOC in these soils may be attributed to slower break down rate (less and constant mineralization rate) and increased above and below ground organic residues due to enhanced crop growth (Moharana *et al.*, 2012). Increase in SOC due to application of organics has also been reported by Dutta *et al.* (2003).

AVAILABLE N, P AND K

Remarkable increase in available N (19.7 to 21.8%) was observed in soils receiving organic nutrients (T_2 to T_6) over the initial status (272.2 to 300.6 kg/ha). The soils treated with inorganics (T_7), on the other hand registered a negative value (– 6.1%) over the initial at the end of 8th cropping cycle (Table 4.8). The gain in available N due to application of organics over inorganic fertilizers (T_7) was in the tune of 38.6 to 65 kg/ha. The increase in available N is attributed to the increase in SOC and might have been partially due to slow release of N from organics (Gami *et al.*, 2001). The buildup of available P in soils receiving organics were 11.0 to 12.2 kg/ha and the increase was by 13.9 to 18.4% over the initial status (9.5 to 10.4 kg/ha). The increase in available P in soils treated with organics might be due to release of organically bound P during decomposition of organic matter. Continuous application of organics also reduced the activity of polyvalent cations such as Ca, Fe and Al due to chelation thereby reducing the P–fixation (Gupta *et al.*, 1988). Soils treated with organics exhibited an increase of available K (16.7 to 20.9%) over the initial value of 118.4 to 123.2 kg/ha, which is attributed to the increased cation exchange capacity due to elevated SOC and thus release of more non exchangeable K from the soil (Blake *et al.*, 1999).

Table 4.8: Changes in soil fertility under organic nutrient management packages in rice–tomato–okra system at Chiplima

Treatment	Initial soil fertility				Soil fertility after 8th crop cycles				% increase or decrease over initial				Average increase over T_7 in 8 yrs			
	OC (g/kg)	N (kg/ha)	P (kg/ha)	K (kg/ha)	OC (g/kg)	N (kg/ha)	P (kg/ha)	K (kg/ha)	OC	N	P	K	OC (g/kg)	N (kg/ha)	P (kg/ha)	K (kg/ha)
T_1	7.43	292.4	10.9	126.4	8.22	319.2	11.6	134.0	10.6	9.2	6.4	6.0	1.29	29.0	3.2	19.6
T_2	7.54	293.2	10.4	123.2	8.89	351.0	11.9	146.4	17.9	19.7	14.4	18.8	1.96	60.8	3.5	32.0
T_3	7.93	300.6	10.1	123.0	9.60	360.8	11.5	143.6	21.1	20.0	13.9	16.7	2.67	70.6	3.1	29.2
T_4	7.63	296.4	10.2	122.3	9.22	355.2	11.8	144.4	20.8	19.8	15.7	18.1	2.29	65.0	3.4	30.0
T_5	7.40	272.2	9.5	118.4	8.80	328.8	11.0	138.6	18.9	20.8	15.8	17.1	1.87	38.6	2.6	24.2
T_6	7.53	285.2	10.3	121.8	9.25	347.5	12.2	147.2	22.8	21.8	18.4	20.9	2.32	57.3	3.8	32.8
T_7	7.78	309.2	9.7	119.4	6.93	290.2	8.4	114.4	–10.9	–6.1	–13.4	–4.2	–	–	–	–
T_8	7.84	304.6	9.8	116.8	8.44	322.6	10.1	131.8	7.7	5.9	3.1	12.8	1.51	32.4	1.7	17.4
Min	7.40	272.2	9.7	116.8	6.93	290.2	8.4	114.4								
Max	7.93	309.2	10.9	126.4	9.60	360.8	11.9	147.2								

Table 4.9: Regression equations on SOC changes under organic nutrient management packages in rice–tomato–okra system at Chiplima

Treatment	Regression equations	R^2
T_1	$Y = 0.089 X^2 - 0.544X + 7.79$	0.9
T_2	$Y = 0.066X^2 - 0.259X + 7.489$	0.988
T_3	$Y = 0.094X^2 - 0.365X + 7.687$	0.985
T_4	$Y = 0.088X^2 - 0.382X + 7.633$	0.975
T_5	$Y = 0.084X^2 - 0.421X + 7.637$	0.986
T_6	$Y = 0.105X^2 - 0.468X + 7.45$	0.995
T_7	$Y = 0.015X^2 - 0.188X + 7.467$	0.490
T_8	$Y = 0.072X^2 - 0.381X + 7.631$	0.954

Table 4.10: Changes in physical properties under organic nutrient management practices in rice–tomato–okra cropping system

Treatments	Initial			After 8th cropping system cycle		
	BD (g/cc)	WHC (%)	SOC (%)	BD (g/cc)	WHC (%)	SOC (%)
T_1	1.46	44.3	0.74	1.43	46.3	0.82
T_2	1.46	44.2	0.75	1.40	48.2	0.90
T_3	1.47	44.9	0.79	1.39	48.9	0.96
T_4	1.46	44.2	0.76	1.41	47.8	0.92
T_5	1.47	44.7	0.74	1.43	46.7	0.88
T_6	1.46	44.0	0.75	1.40	48.5	0.93
T_7	1.46	44.4	0.78	1.46	45.2	0.69
T_8	1.47	43.9	0.78	1.44	46.1	0.84

BD, bulk density; WHC, water holding capacity.

MICROBIAL POPULATION

The initial and final (after 8th cropping cycle) population of bacteria, fungi and actinomycetes is presented in table 4.11. The soils receiving organic nutrients (T_2 to T_6) registered the maximum increase of bacteria (32.4 to 37.1%), fungi (30.2 to 34.4%) and actinomycetes (29.3 to 35.9%) population over the initial status. The soils under inorganic nutrients (T_7), however exhibited minimum increase in microbial communities with values of 11.2, 5.5 and 11.2% for bacteria, fungi and actinomycetes, respectively. Increased organic carbon content of the soil due to application of various organic nutrients over the years served as a source of energy for biological activity thereby enhancing the density of microbes (Singh *et al.*, 2008). Further, most of the soil microorganisms are chemo–autotrophs, which require organic source of carbon as food and oxidation of organic substances provides energy, this might be the reason in improving microbial population in soils under organics (Ingle *et al.*, 2014).

Table 4.11: Changes in microbial attributes under organic nutrient management packages in rice–tomato–okra system at Chiplima

Treatment	Initial status of microbial attributes				Status of microbial attributes after 8th crop cycles				% increase or decrease over initial				Average increase over T_7 in 8 years			
	Microbial population			MBC µg C/g	Microbial population			MBC µg C/g	Microbial population			MBC				MBC µg C/g
	Bacteria cfu×10^7	Fungi cfu×10^4	Actinomycetes cfu×10^6		Bacteria cfu×10^7	Fungi cfu×10^4	Actinomycetes cfu×0^6		Bacteria	Fungi	Actinomycetes		Bacteria cfu×10^7	Fungi cfu×10^4	Actinomycetes cfu×10^6	
T_1	20.3	13.2	12.6	108.3	25.2	15.4	14.9	143.3	24.1	16.7	18.3	32.3	2.3	1.9	1.0	23.0
T_2	22.1	12.7	12.8	112.4	29.7	16.7	17.1	179.3	34.4	31.5	33.6	59.5	6.8	3.2	3.2	59.0
T_3	21.5	12.8	13.2	115.7	28.9	17.0	17.3	182.3	34.4	32.8	31.1	57.6	6.0	3.5	3.4	62.0
T_4	19.7	13.0	12.5	104.7	26.9	17.3	16.8	168.3	36.5	33.1	34.4	60.7	4.0	3.8	2.9	48.3
T_5	20.7	12.9	13.3	111.3	27.4	16.8	17.2	170.7	32.4	30.2	29.3	53.4	4.5	3.3	3.3	50.4
T_6	21.3	13.1	12.8	118.2	29.2	17.6	17.4	191.3	37.1	34.4	35.9	61.8	6.3	4.1	3.5	71.0
T_7	20.6	12.8	12.5	107.7	22.9	13.5	13.9	120.3	11.2	5.5	11.2	11.7	–	–	–	–
T_8	22.1	12.6	12.6	105.3	26.4	14.4	14.8	137.3	19.5	14.3	17.5	30.4	3.5	0.9	0.9	17.0
Min	19.7	12.6	12.5	105.3	22.9	13.5	13.9	120.3								
Max	22.1	13.2	13.3	118.2	29.7	17.6	17.4	191.3								

MBC, microbial biomass carbon; cfu, colony forming units.

SOIL MICROBIAL BIOMASS CARBON

Microbial biomass carbon (MBC) like soil organic carbon (SOC) has been included in the current soil monitoring concept due to its rapid response and high sensitivity to management practices and environmental changes (Neogi *et al.*, 2014). The microbial biomass carbon of the soils under organic nutrients was enhanced considerably (+53.4% to +61.8%) over the initial contents of 104.7 to 118.2 µg C/g. The soils under inorganic fertilization (T_7) on the other hand registered the minimum gain (+ 8.7%) in MBC over the initial (107.7 µg C/g). The higher MBC in soils receiving organics is related to higher microbial population due to balanced supply of nutrients and carbon (Basak *et al.*, 2012). The good quality organic inputs with lower doses of chemical fertilizers have a potential to augment soil enzymes activities and improve the microbial biomass carbon and organic carbon (Nath *et al.*, 2012).

The microbial quotient (ratio of MBC to SOC) is considered to be a more useful measure of change in soil biological processes than either microbial biomass C or organic C individually (Anderson and Domsch, 1989). The higher MBC/SOC ratio of 1.83 to 2.07 in soils under organics can be explained by increased substrate availability to microorganisms provided through the higher buildup of SOC (Jacobs *et al.*, 2009).

CONCLUSION

Application of $1/3^{rd}$ N each through FYM, green manuring of *dhaincha* and neem cake + *Azospirillum* + PSB to rice followed by similar combination of FYM, vermi–compost, neem cake + *Azotobacter* + PSB to both tomato and okra is the best organic nutrient management practice in rice–tomato–okra system for improving soil health and productivity in Alfisols in the Hirakud command area under West Central Table Land zone of Odisha.

REFERENCES

Anderson, T.H. and Domsch, K.H. 1989. Ratios of Microbial Biomass Carbon to Total Carbon in Arable Soils. *Soil Biology and Biochemistry* 21: 471-479.

Basak, B.B., Biswas, D.R. and Rattan, R.K. 2012. Comparative Effectiveness of Value added Manures on Crop Productivity, Soil Mineral Nitrogen and Soil Carbon Pools under Maize–Wheat Cropping System in an Inceptisol. *Journal of the Indian Society of Soil Science* 60: 288-98.

Blake, L., Mercik, S., Koerschens, M., Goulding, K.W.T., Stempen, S., Weigel, A., Poulton., P.R. and Powlson, D.S. 1999. Potassium Content in Soil, uptake in Plants and the Potassium Balance in Three European Long-term Field Experiments. *Plant Soil* 216: 1-14.

Dhingra, O.P. and Sinclair, J.B. 1993. *Basic Plant Pathology Methods*, CBS Publishers, Delhi. 179-180.

Dubey, R., Sharma, R.S. and Dubey, D.P. 2014. Effect of Organic, Inorganic and Integrated Nutrient Management on Crop Productivity, Water Productivity and Soil Properties under Various Rice–based Cropping Systems in Madhya Pradesh, India. *International Journal of Current Microbiology and Applied Sciences* 3(2): 381-389.

Dutta, S., Pal, R., Chakraborty, A. and Chakrabarti, K. 2003. Influence of Integrated Plant Nutrient Supply System on Soil Quality Restoration in a Red and Laterite Soil. *Archives of Agronomy and Soil Science* 49: 631-637.

Gami, S.K., Ladha, J.K., Pathak, H., Shah, M.P., Pasuquin, E., Pandey, S.P., Hobbs, P.R., Joshy, D., and Mishra, R., 2001. Long-term Changes in yield and Soil Fertility in a20-year Rice–Wheat Experiment in Nepal. *Biology and Fertility of Soils* 34: 73-78.

Gangwar, B. and Ram, B. 2005. Effect of Crop Diversification on Productivity and Profitability of Rice (*Oryza sativa*)–wheat (*Triticum aestivum*) System. *Indian Journal of Agricultural Sciences* 75(7): 435-438.

Gupta, A.P., Antil, R.S. and Narwal, R.P. 1988. Effect of Farmyard Manure on Organic Carbon, available N, and P Content of Soil during Different Periods of Wheat Growth. *Journal of Indian Society of Soil Science* 36(2): 269-273.

Ingle, S.S., Jadhao, S.D., Kharche, V.K., Sonune, B.A. and Mali, D.V. 2014. Soil Biological Properties as Influenced by Long–term Manuring and Fertilization under Sorghum (*Sorghum bicolor*)–Wheat (*Triticum aestivum*) Sequence in Vertisols. *Indian Journal of Agricultural Sciences* 84: 452-457.

Jacobs, A., Rauber, R. and Ludwig, B. 2009. Impact of Reduced Tillage on Carbon and Nitrogen Storage of Two *Haplic Luvisols* after 40 years. *Soil and Tillage Research* 102: 158-164.

John, P.S., Georg, M. and Jacob, R. 2001. Nutrient Mining in Agro–climatic Zones of Kerala. *Fertilizer News* 46: 45-52, 55-57.

Knudsen, D., Peterson, G.A. and Pratt, P.F. 1982. Lithium, Sodium and Potassium. *In:* Page, A.L., Miller, R.H., Keeney, D.R. (Eds.). Part-II, *Chemical and Microbiological Properties*. 2nd Edition. American Society of Agronomy and Soil Science Society of America, Madison, USA: 228-238.

Kumpawat, B.S. 2001. Production Potential and Economics of Different Crop Sequences. *Indian Journal of Agronomy* 46(3): 421-424.

Meena, K.N., Ashok Kumar, Rana, D.S. and Meena, N.C. 2011. Productivity and Nutrient uptake of Maize (*Zea mays*)–Wheat (*Triticum aestivum*) Cropping System under Different Biosources and Nitrogen Levels. *Indian Journal of Agronomy* 56 (3): 182-188.

Moharana, P.C., Sharma, B.M., Biswas, D.R., Dwivedi, B.S. and Singh, R.V. 2012. Long–term Effect of Nutrient Management on Soil Fertility and Soil Organic Carbon Pools Under a 6-year-old Pearl Millet–Wheat Cropping System in an *Inceptisol* of Subtropical India. *Field Crops Research* 136: 32-41.

Nath, D.J., Ozah, B., Baruah, R., Barooah, R.C., Borah, D.K., and Gupta, M. 2012. Soil Enzymes and Microbial Biomass Carbon under Rice–*toria* Sequence as Influenced by Nutrient Management. *Journal of the Indian Society of Soil Science* 60(1): 20-24.

Neogi, S., Bhattacharyya, P., Roy, K.S., Panda, B.B., Nayak, A.K., Rao, K.S. and Manna, M.C. 2014. Soil Respiration, Labile Carbon Pools, and Enzyme Activities as Affected by Tillage Practices in a Tropical Rice–maize–cowpea Cropping System. *Environmental Monitoring and Assessment* 186: 4223-4236.

Ngwira, A., Sleutel, S. and DeNeve, S. 2012. Soil Carbon Dynamics as Influenced by Tillage and Crop Residue Management in Loamy Sand and Sandy Loam Soils under Smallholder Farmers' Conditions in Malawi. *Nutrient Cycling in Agroecosystems* 92: 315-328.

Olsen, S.R., Cole, C.V., Watenabe, F.S. and Dean, L.R. 1954. Estimation of Available Phosphorus in Soils by Extraction with Sodium Bicarbonate. *USDA Circular 939*.

Patnaik, S. and Rao, M.V. 1979. Sources of Nitrogen for Rice Production. *In*: *Nitrogen and Rice*. IRRI, Los Banos, Philippines.

Porpavai, S., Devasenapathy, P., Siddeswaran, K. and Jayaraj, T. 2011. Impact of Various Rice based Cropping Systems on Soil Fertility. *Journal of Cereals and Oilseeds* 2(3): 43-46.

Pramanik, S.C. and Ravisankar, N. 2007. Productivity, Profitability and Sustainability of Rice-based Cropping Systems in Bay Islands. *Journal of Farming Systems Research and Development* 13(1): 93-98.

Rao, A.U., Murthy, K.M.D., Sridhar, T.V., Raju, S.K. and Lakshmi, D.A. 2014. Studies on Performance of Organic Farming and Chemical Farming in Rainy Season Rice. *International Journal of Plant, Animal and Environmental Sciences* 4(4): 202-206.

Rupela, O.P., Humayun, P., Venkateswarlu, B. and Yadav, A.K. 2006. Comparing Conventional and Organic Farming Crop Production Systems: Inputs, Minimal Treatments and Data Needs. *Organic Farming Newsletter* 2: 3-17.

Shalini Pilai, P., Geethakumari, V.L. and Sheeba Rebecca, I. 2007. Balance–sheet of Soil Nitrogen in Rice (*Oryza sativa*)-based Cropping Systems under Integrated Nutrient Management. *Indian Journal of Agronomy* 52(1): 16-20.

Sharma, A.K., Thakur, N.P., Kaur, M. and Kumar, P. 2007. Profitable and Energy Efficient Rice–based Cropping System under Sub–tropical Irrigated Conditions of Jammu. *Journal of Farming System Research and Development* 13(1): 128-130.

Sharma, R.P., Pathak, S.K. and Raman, K.R. 2004. Diversification of Traditional Rice–based Cropping System for Sustainable Production in South Bihar Alluvial Plains. Indian Journal of Agronomy 49(4): 218-222.

Singh, A.B., Ramesh, P., Panwar, N.R. and Ramana, S. 2008. Nutritional Quality of Soybean (*Glycin max*), Wheat (*Triticum durum*) and Chickpea (*Cicer arietinum*) and Soil Biological Properties as Influenced by Different Organic Manures. *Indian Journal of Agricultural Sciences* 78: 781-784.

Singh, R.P., Das, S.K., Bhaskar Rao, U.M. and Narayana Reddy, M. 1990. *Towards Sustainable Dryland Agricultural Practices*. Bulletin, Published by CRIDA, Hyderabad.

Subbiah, B.V. and Asija, C.L. 1956. A Rapid Procedure for the Estimation of Available N in Soils. *Current Science* 25: 328.

Tiwari, K.N. 2001. Nutrient Removal by Crops. *Fertilizer Knowledge No.1.* Potash and Phosphate Institute of Canada–India Programme, Gurgaon, India.

Vance, E.D., Brookes, P.C. and Jenkinson, D.S. 1987. An Extraction method for Measuring Soil Microbial Biomass Carbon. *Soil Biology and Biochemistry* 19: 703-707.

Walkley, A. and Black, I.A. 1934. An Examination of the Degtjareff method for Determining Soil Organic Matter and a Proposed Modification of the Chromic Acid Titration method. *Soil Science* 37: 29-38.

Pages: 74-88

Irrigation Practices and Sustainable Agriculture
Edited by: **Dr. Prasann Kumar and Dr. Pawan Kumar 'Bharti'**
ISBN: 978-93-88854-31-3
Edition: **2020**
Published by: **Discovery Publishing House Pvt. Ltd., New Delhi (India)**

5

Water Use Efficiency with Special Reference to Stress of Salinity

Prasann Kumar[1, 2*], Johnson Yumnam[1]

GRAPHICAL ABSTRACT

Keywords: Abiotic, Efficiency, Stress, Water, Use

INTRODUCTION

The biotic and abiotic stress effects on the growth and development of plants. Water stress and cold stress restricted plant growth. MicroRNAs

[1] Department of Agronomy, School of Agriculture, Lovely Professional University, Jalandhar - 144 411 (Punjab) (India)
[2] Divison of Research and Development, Lovely Professional University, Jalandhar - 144 411 (Punjab) (India)

are so called miRNAs which are endogenous and have approximate 22 nucleotide, small non-coding regulatory RNAs that play important role in the plant. Salt stress significantly reduced the dry matter content of roots, stems, leaves and leaf area. NaCl increases plant height with low and medium concentrations and deceases with higher concentration. Number of leaves and leaf areas, osmotic potential decreases with higher concentrations of it. Deficiency of Phosphorus is a major limitation to N_2 fixation. As the supply of P increased, the number of leaves, leaf area, and dry weight also increases. Under salinity conditions, N application cause ameliorative effect on genotype, dry weight, physio-biochemical parameters such as present water content, net photosynthetic rate, stomatal conductance, total chlorophyll. Grain legumes contain numerous phytochemicals useful for their nutritional or nutraceutical properties, such as tocopherols prevent cardiovascular disease and eye pathologies. Abiotic stress responses include change in physiological, biochemical, morphological and developmental processes. ROS controls architectural change in stressed seedlings. Silicon is second most abundant element both on surface of earth's crust and in soils. The beneficial role of Si in stimulating the growth and development of many plant. ROS formation and scavenging become unbalanced, and oxidative damage may occur. Harpin protein induces disease resistance in diverse plant. Calcium ions play a role as a second messenger in mediating various defense responses under environmental stresses. The biotic and abiotic stress effects on the growth and development of plants. Abiotic stress includes salt concentration, drought conditions, temperatures, heavy metal toxicity etc. On the other hand biotic stress includes damages by living organisms such as bacteria, viruses, fungi, parasites. In these situations plant is growing in a non-ideal growth conditions. Stress effects lead to deficiencies in growth, crop yield, permanent damage or death.

ISOLATION AND EXPRESSION ANALYSIS OF NOVEL ABIOTIC STRESS-INDUCED GENE W89 FROM WHEAT

Water stress and cold stress restricted plant growth. A putative water stress-induced gene, W89, was clones from the cDNA ofdrought-treated wheat seedlings. Its entire length was obtained using 5′-rapid amplification of cDNA ends. It was supposed that W89 was novel dehydration-responsive protein encoding gene. Drought stress resulted in water loss from plant cells. It's difficult for plant to consume moisture because of the osmotic imbalance due to high salt and cold stress which may lead to physiological disorders.

Crop water use and water use efficiency on irrigated cotton farm: Irrigation efficiency (IE) water use efficiency is important for gaining maximum return from a limited resource.

Efficiency of water use on cotton properties into two components:

- Irrigation efficiency: proportion of irrigation and rainfall input to the farm for production of cotton
- Crop water use efficiency (CWUE): the amount of lint produced per unit of water used by the crop as ET.
- In Australia irrigated cotton is grown in laser graded fields using surface/furrow irrigation.

THE EFFECT OF ARBUSCULAR MYCORRHIZAL FUNGI (AMF) ON REACTIVE OXYRADICAL SCAVENGING SYSTEM OF TOMATO UNDER SALT TOLERANCE

Salt stress significantly reduced the dry matter content of roots, stems, leaves and leaf area. The effect is more in aerial biomass then in root biomass which is due to AM colonization. The activities of SOD, POD, ASA-POD, and CAT increased and have different rules under different salt stress conditions but there is a rise of enzymes in the beginning of treatment under salt stress conditions. Tomato is a major vegetable plant and is sensitive to salinity (Ayres and Westcot 1985). The AMF inoculums consisted of spores, soil, hyphae and infected clove root fragment (denoted by tuned tackas).

IMPROVING TOLERANCE TO ABIOTIC STRESSES IN RAINFED LOW LAND RICE

The most severe constraints to productivity are amount and timing of water supply. Higher rainfall and poor drainage can rise water depths in rice filed that submerge rice plants lead to severe yield loss. These type of areas are low in soil fertility and soil nutrients and depend on water availability. To increase yield stability and reliability of response to improved crop management we need to improve tolerance of rice to both drought and submergence.The main factor drought affects crop grain yield. According to Gregory *et.al.* (1997) the ratio of total biomass produced against total available water may be expressed as:

$$WUE_8 = \frac{M}{E_S + T + R + D}$$

Water stress at critical growth stages, excessive soil water evaporation, soil water storage, runoff, and drainage are among the factors which decline in ratios of economic yield: evapotranspiration or water use efficiency and economic yield. Basically these terms are used to promote the efficient use of irrigation water at crop production levels.Water use efficiency can be defined as the ratio of economic yield(Y) to evaporation (ET), given as $WUE=YET^{-1}$. The maximum yields were similar in 1998 and 1999, but the maximum seasonal ETs were not similar. Stewart and Hargan (1973) found that the maximum yield was based on varietal characteristics alone, while maximum ET was dependent upon environment.

PLANT miRNAs AND ABIOTIC STRESS RESPONSES

MicroRNAs are so called miRNAs which are endogenous and have approximate 22 nucleotide (nt) small non-coding regulatory RNAs that play important role in the plant. This may done by targeting mRNAs for cleavage or translational repression.

microRNAs (SHORT-INTERFERING RNAs)

- 20-24 nucleotide
- Single standard RNAs
- Known by miRNAs
- Play important regulatory Roles in plant.
- Effect on organ development like leaf morphogenesis, floral Organ identity, root development. Abiotic stresses, such as drought, salinity and extreme temperatures, regulate the expression of thousands of genes in plants at both transcriptional and posttranscriptional levels.

MiRNAs involved in: dehydration, mineral-nutrient, mechanical stress.

PHOSPHORUS EFFICIENCY OF WILD AND CULTIVATED GENOTYPES

Deficiency of Phosphorus is a major limitation to N_2 fixation. As the supply of P increased, the number of leaves, leaf area, and dry weight also increases. Weedy and wild genotypes are used as source of resistance to diseases and pests, soil constraints, and genetic diversity.

PHYSIOLOGY OF LEGUME NODULE AND ITS RESPONSE TO STRESS

With the decrease nodule cortical permeability, there is a primary limitation of O_2 supply to the infected zone during environmental stress. Cortical cell turgor is influenced by balance of solutes between the apoplast and symplast. Variations in phloem supply may occur due to stress events. Or soluble sugar and nitrogenous solutes content is changed due to decrease in rate of N_2 fixation.Change in cortical cell turgor may affect the turgor gradient driving phloem supply into nodule in form of turgor homeostat. Nodule anatomy and physiology is heterogenous.

EFFECT OF SALT STRESS ON PLANT GROWTH AND METABOLISM

NaCl increases plant height with low and medium concentrations and deceases with higher concentration. Number of leaves and leaf areas, osmotic potential decreases with higher concentrations of it. Salinity increased both fresh and dry weights of the shoot. Salinity may decrease chlorophyll content. Due to salinity stress there is increase in protein content. Salinity of the soil limits spread of plants in their natural habitats. From the population 40% may die due to highest concentrations. The measurements taken are:

- Length of the shoot system
- Number of plant leaves
- Leaf area
- Fresh and dry weight of the plant
- Protein was determined by Lowry method.

  Effect of salt stress on internal water relations:
- Osmotic potential of leaf sap

  Effect of salt stress on chemical content:
- Photosynthetic pigments
- Protein content

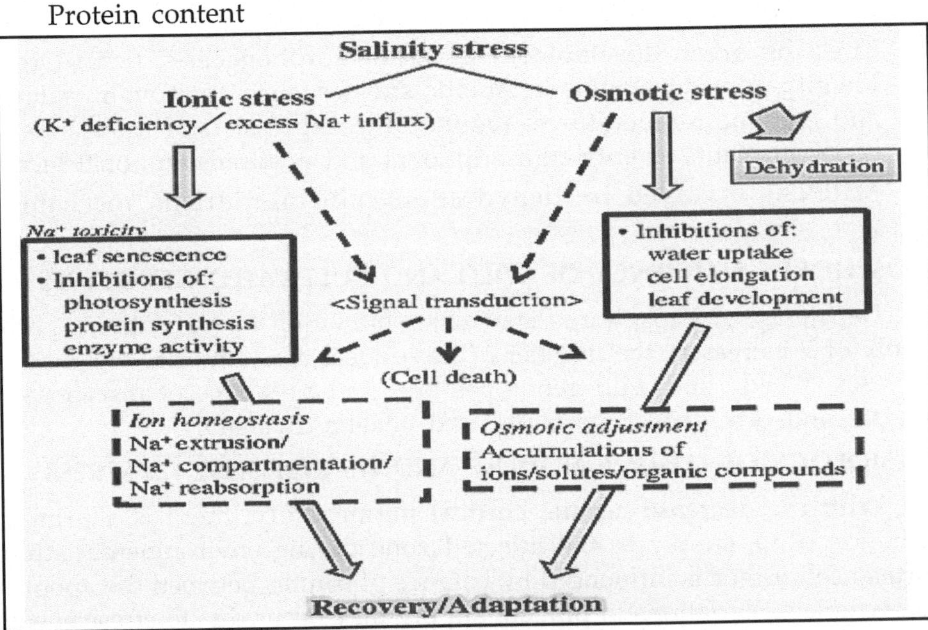

Fig. 5.1: Salinity stress

Source: based on review of literature

HYDROXYPROLINE-RICH PLANT GLYCOPROTEINS

Broad group of glycosylated protein which are characterized by the proline/hydroxyproline content of the protein backbone and the fact that the glycosyl components contain arabinose and galactose as major monosaccharides. These glycoproteins and proteoglycans are known as hydroxyproline-rich glycoprotein (HRGPs). They are reported in a number of unicellular algae. The protein backbones, being heavily glycosylated and rich in proline, are not readily amenable to direct protein sequencing. There are multiple codons for each of these amino acids which had made cDNA cloning based on PCR very difficult. cDNA cloning is also complicated by deletions, rearrangements, and hybrid formation during preparation of the libraries.

NITROGEN IN RELATION TO PHOTOSYNTHETIC CAPACITY AND ACCUMULATION OF OSMOPROTECTANT AND NUTRIENTS

Under salinity conditions, N application cause ameliorative effect on genotype, dry weight, physio-biochemical parameters such as present water content, net photosynthetic rate, stomatal conductance, total chlorophyll, carbonic anhydrase activity and malondialdehyde, nitrogen, potassium and sodium content etc. and yield attributes. Salinity stress affects the crop productivity. Saline environment deficient in Nitrogen (Amonkar and Karmarkar 1995) and reduction in NO_3^- uptake could be mostly due to high Cl^- content in soil. Ion and osmotic homeostasis is necessary for plant to be salt tolerant. Plant subjected to salinity accumulate no of nitrogen containing compounds (NCC) such as amino acid, amides, imino acids and proteins, quaternary ammonium compounds and polyamines. NCC have pivotal roles in osmotic adjustments, protection of cellular macromolecules, storage from of nitrogen, maintenance of cellular Ph, detoxification of the cells, and scavenging of free radicals.

LEGUMES ARE VALUABLE SOURCES OF TOCOPHEROLS

Grain legumes contain numerous phytochemicals useful for their nutritional or nutraceutical properties, such as tocopherols prevent cardiovascular disease and eye pathologies. Gamma congener was the most abundant tocopherol and delta-tocopherol. Legumes contains health promoting components, such as fiber, proteins, resistant starch, minerals and numerous phytochemicals. Hydrophilic phytochemicals, such as ascorbic acid, phenolic acids and polyphenols these may enhancement of immune system functionality and reduce cancer risk, whereas lipophilic phytonutrients, such as carotenoids and tocopherols, may prevent the risk of cardiovascular diseases. Tocopherols behave as potent antioxidants. The word "vitamin E" indicates both tocopherols and tocotrienols. Both tocopherols and tocotrienols exist in four different congeners (vitamers) called alpha, beta, gamma and delta. In humans, vitamin E deficiencies do not lead to a characteristic disease state or disorder. The composition of tocopherols in food is complex and the biological activity of each congener depends on its specific structure, the most useful parameter to compare different food items in the vitamin E activity.

BASES FOR GENETIC IMPROVEMENT OF GRAIN LEGUMES

Among the food legumes, soybean is the only crop where consistent improvements in yield.

BREEDING METHODOLOGIES

In grain legumes, like other species, the plant breeding process include four stages:

- Planning and hybridization
- Early generation selection
- Line evaluation
- Variety release

Singh (1989) has classified genetic resources into three categories:

1. Basic genetic resources
2. Derived genetic resources
3. Genetic resources at molecular levels.

Choice of parents is a starting material to be used in breeding program. Choice of breeding method depends on different items:

1. The reproductive system
2. The genetics of the trait
3. Environment-genotype interactions
4. The final product of the breeder's work.

RESPONSES OF CONTRASTING RICE GENOTYPES TO SALT STRESS

Study was conducted to investigate the effects of applying different concentrations of the macronutrients K^+, Ca^{2+}, and Mg^2 on responses of contrasting rice genotypes under salt stress.

The tolerant genotypes had higher concentration of k in their shoots and greater root and shoot biomass and green leaf area. the active and developing tissues of tolerant genotypes maintain much lower concentration of nutrients. Calcium is particularly more effective both magnesium and potassium, and can be applied at relatively larger quantities in salt affected soils. Salt stress reduces the growth and productivity of crop plants and In severe cases may lead to complete mortality (Munna and Tester 2008). As rice is sensitive to salt stress during seedling and reproductive stages but relatively tolerant during germination, active tillering and grain filling (pearson and Ayers 1960).

SALT STRESS AFFECTS GLUTAMINE SYNTHETASE ACTIVITY AND MRNA ACCUMULATION ON POTATO PLANTS

Assimilation of ammonium into glutamine and glutamate is vital for plant growth as these are precursors for almost all nitrogenous compounds. Ammonium may also be directly incorporated into glutamate by the glutamate dehydrogenase aminating reactive. Potato is tolerant to salinity. Potato GS is encoded by a small multigene family. When potato exposed to salt stress, increased ammonium assimilation occurs in roots, due to an increased GS accumulation, along with a decreased assimilation in leaves. Plant distribution and productivity reduces due to environmental stresses such as drought, salinity and low or high temperatures. Plants with roots grow in salty water, losing enormous volumes of water. The effects of salinity on plant nitrogen metabolism studies to date revealed increased protein degradation, inhibition of protein synthesis and accumulation/ Degradation of protein and non-protein amino acids in a small group of dicots and monocots.

PROTECTIVE ROLE OF EXOGENOUS NITRIC OXIDE AGAINST OXIDATIVE-STRESS INDUCED BY SALT STRESS

Salt stress increase ion leakage, lipid peroxidation and protein oxidation in barley leaves. The presence of nitric oxide donor increased the activities of superoxide dismutase, ascorbate peroxidases, and catalases. Sodium nitroprusside addition increased accumulation of ferritin at protein level, indicating that nitric oxide directly regulated ferritin accumulation. Nitric oxide can effectively protect seedlings from salt stress damage by enhancing activities of antioxidant enzymes. High salinity cause plant death or decrease productivity. It may also affect plant processes such as photosynthesis, protein synthesis, energy, and lipid metabolism. Salt stress affects plants by causing ion imbalance and hyperosmotic stress. Presence of NO induce seed germination, to affect growth and development, to increase iron homeostasis, to regulate plant maturation and senescence, and to medicate abscisic acid (ABA)-induced stomatal closing, and NO protects plant from oxidative stresses. The production of malendialdehyde (MDA) is used as a indicator of membrane lipid peroxidation, another indicator of stress in plant membrane. In high salt conditions, plant activate a number of antioxidant enzymes that protect against potentially cytotoxic reactive oxygen species (ROS).

PROTEIN COMPONENTS OF PULSES AND THEIR POTENTIAL IMPACT ON HUMAN HEALTH

Pulses may contain a number of bioactive substances include enzymes inhibitors, lectins, phytates, oligosaccharides, and phenolic compounds. Enzyme inhibitors can diminish protein digestibility, and lectins can reduce nutrient absorption, but have little effect on cooking. Phytic acid can diminish mineral bio-availability. Flatulence is caused by galactooligosaccharides. Phytic acid exhibit antioxidant activity and protects DNA damage, phenolic compounds have antioxidant. These compounds can have complementary and overlapping mechanisms of action, including modulation of detoxifying enzymes, stimulation of the immune system, regulation of lipid and hormone metabolism, antioxidant, antimutagen, and antiangiogenic effects, reduction of tumor initiation, and promotion and induction of apoptosis. Secondary metabolites are considerated antinutrients, simultaneously conferring health benefits, so these secondary metabolites are currently marketed as functional foods and nutraceuticals ingredients. Pulses grains are high in protein, carbohydrates, dietary, fiber and rich source of other nutritional components. Same compounds may have protective effects against cancer. Phytic acid has antioxidant and DNA protective effects.

ENZYMES OF C_4 PHOTOSYNTHESIS

Non-photosynthetic counterparts of these enzymes,maintenance of pH and replenishment of Krebs cycle intermediates, thereby contributing to the biosynthesis of amino acids and other compounds and providing NADPH for biosynthesis and the antioxidant system. The activities of all of these enzymes were enhanced in plants under biotic stress caused by viral infection. Resistance mechanisms that allow plants to avoid or tolerate stress are activated either by acclimatization and adaptation. photosynthetic efficiency depends on the activity of ribulose-1,5-bisphoshatecarboxylase/ oxygenase. When the atmospheric CO_2 decreased and O_2 increased, CO_2 concentration mechanisms (CCMs) evolved to reduce photorespiration. PEPC is also involved in the regulation of pH and electroneutrality. An increase in cytoplasmic pH increases the activity of PEPC. PEPC is one of the CO_2-fixing enzymes that irreversibly catalysis the carboxylation of phosphoenolpyruvate in the presence of HCO_3 and a divalent metal ion (Mg_2+, Mn_2+) to yield oxaloacetate and Pi. This reaction is highly exergonic.

WOUND-INDUCED PHENOLIC ACCUMULATION AND BROWNING IN LETTUCE IS REDUCED BY EXPOSURE TO N-ALCOHOLS

Wound originate at site of injury in lettuce leaf tissue and propagates into adjacent tissuewhere it induces a number of physiological responses which include increased phenolic metabolism. Wounding increases phenolic metabolism in lettuce leaf tissue with the production and accumulation of soluble phenolic compounds that subsequently react to produce wound-induced tissue browning.

MORPH GENIC EFFECTS OF ABIOTIC STRESS AND ADAPTATION TO HOT SPRING

Abiotic stress responses include change in physiological, biochemical, morphological and developmental processes. ROS controls architectural change in stressed seedlings. Mechanisms evolved that diminish the impact of stresses on plant growth and development is called protective responses and are highly stress-specific. phytochelatins specifically remove heavy metals from the cytoplasm. Enzymatic scavengers of free reactive oxygen species (ROS) like superoxide dismutase, catalase, and ascorbate peroxidase, or low molecular weight antioxidants like ascorbate (ASC) and glutathione (GSH), prevent oxidative damage. Growth and productivity reduced by exposure to temperatures in excess. Leaves developed during exposure to elevated temperatures had reduced thickness. Plants isolated from thermal environments also had greater number of stomata. Adaptive responses occur at many levels of plant organization (Feder and Hofmann, 1999) and include heritable changes in stomatal physiology (Radin *et al.*, 1994), increased photorespiration (Weis and Berry, 1988), altered fatty acid content of chloroplast membranes (Murakami *et al.*, 2000), enhanced resistance to loss of intrinsic protein structure.

GENERATION AND SCAVENGING OF ROS IN CHLOROPLAST

The specific traits of oxygen chemistry are examined as a basis of the step-wise electron acceptance by O_2, giving rise to incompletely reduced highly reactive oxygen species (ROS) comprising both free radical and non-radicalforms (H_2O_2). The reversal of electron spin of oxygen, induced by energy transfer from triplet state chlorophyll, is considered as a generator of another non-radical ROS, singlet oxygen $O_{2.}$ ROS are primarily agents of damage. Chloroplasts are the major source of ROS. The electron carriers for ROS include Fe-S clusters and ferredoxin in PSI, and Q_A and Q_B in PSII. Stress factors limiting CO_2 fixation and hence decreasing NADPH utilization and NADP regeneration exacerbate high-light stress; ROS formation and scavenging become unbalanced, and oxidative damage may occur. A particularly important plant process that is affected by stress is photosynthesis. The balance between these inseparable facets is of vital importance for the survival and normal functioning of aerobic organism.ROS, resulting from electron transfers and energyinput to oxygen, are distinguished by high chemical activity. They play a versatile role as factors of damage, protection or signaling depending on the delicate equilibrium between ROS production and scavenging at the proper site and time, i.e. on their fine spatial and temporal regulation. Uncontrolled production or inefficient scavenging of ROS in chloroplasts arising in stress conditions.

CALCIUM IONS ARE INVOLVED IN THE DELAY OF PLANT CELL CYCLE PROGRESSION BY ABIOTIC STRESSES

Calcium ions play a role as a second messenger in mediating various defense responses under environmental stresses. Role of it on cell cycle progression under abiotic stresses noticed in tobacco BY-2 suspension culture cells. Oxidative and hypoosmotic stress both induce an increase of intracellular calcium and cause a delay of the cell cycle. Some experiments revealed that increase in cytoplasmic calcium concentration serves as second messenger to mediate defense responses. During plant cell cycle progression, oxidative stress is known to impair G_1/S transition to slow down DNA replication and to delay the initiation of mitosis.

HERBACEOUS VEGETATION

Herbaceous plant cover, plant biomass, plant density are higher under a tree canopy and this positive interactions still increase with higher abiotic stress conditions.

TAMING ABIOTIC STRESS IN PLANTS THROUGH GENETIC ENGINEERING

Comai *et al.* produced transgenic tobacco plants showing enhanced resistance to glyphosate through over-expression of the altered enol pyruvyl shikimate 3-phosphate synthase gene. Abel *et al.* raised transgenic tobacco plants overexpressing the coat protein gene of the tobacco mosaic virus, for enhanced virus resistance. Abiotic stresses adversely affect almost all major field-grown plants belonging to varied ecosystems. The severity of abiotic stresses is on the rise due to intensive cultivation being practiced in the farming areas as well as due to environmental deterioration caused by the greenhouse effect. Cause a great amount of loss, both in terms of biomass as well as economic return.Tolerance to abiotic stresses so far has mainly been achieved through engineering for increased cellular levels of osmotically-active solutes. Increased levels of osmolytes has often enhanced tolerance for water stress, salt stress and cold stress at the same time implying that genetic engineering by altering osmolytes is a fruitful approach for obtaining combined tolerance to different abiotic stresses.

LEAF ROLLING BY BIOTIC AND ABIOTIC STRESS FACTOR

Leaf rolling is known as a typical response to water deficit in numerous species such as rice, maize, wheat and sorghum. It occurs not only from water deficit nut also due to abiotic stress factors such as salt, temperatures, heavy metal and UV radiation. In addition to the abiotic factors, herbivores, viruses, bacteria and fungi are biotic factors of leaf rolling. Leaf rolling is an effective protective mechanism from the effects of high light levels in agricultural fields and protects leaves of unirrigated plants from photodamage. The rolling reduces effective leaf area and transpiration, and thus is a potentially useful drought avoidance mechanism in dry areas. Leafrolling is a hydronastic mechanism that reduces light interception, transpiration and leafdehydration. Leaf rolling might play a similar role in osmotic adjustment to maintaining internal plant water status. In the case of mid-season drought, high level of leaf rolling can be advantageous in terms of prevention of water loss and excess radiation. Moreover photosynthesis is affected highly by drought stress. Leaf rolling during stress reduced the leaf surface exposing to sun light energy and transpiration leading to closure of stomata, thus CO_2 entry into cells reduced and photosynthesis also decreased.

Abiotic stress factors causing leaf rolling:

- water deficit
- temperature
- irradiation

Biotic stress factors causing leaf rolling:

- insects
- viruses
- fungi
- bacteria

MECHANISMS OF SILICON-MEDIATED ALLEVIATION OF BIOTIC STRESSES IN HIGHER PLANTS

Silicon is second most abundant element both on surface of earth's crust and in soils. The beneficial role of Si in stimulating the growth and development of many plant. Silicon is known to effectively mitigate various abiotic stresses such as manganese, aluminum and heavy metal toxicities. Silicon is present as silicic acid in the soil solution at concentrations normally ranging from 0.1 to 0.6 mm. The key mechanisms of Si-mediated alleviation of abiotic stresses in higher plants include:

1. Stimulation of antioxidant systems in plants;
2. Complexation or co-precipitation of toxic metal ions with Si;
3. Immobilization of toxic metal ions in growth media;
4. Uptake processes; and
5. Compartmentation of metal ions within plants. Future salinity, drought, chilling and freezing stresses.

It is beneficial for the healthy growth and development of many plant species.

An element is essential that fulfils either one or both of the following criteria:

1. The element is part of a molecule which is an intrinsic component of the structure or metabolism of the plant; and
2. The plant can be so severely deficient in the element that it exhibits abnormalities in growth, development, or reproduction.

In general, gramineous plants take up much more Si than other species, while most dicotyledonous plants absorb Si passively and some dicots such as legumes exclude Si from uptake (Ma *et al.*, 2001a; Liang *et al.*, 2005b).

CONCLUSION

Drought stress resulted in water loss from plant cells. It's difficult for plant to consume moisture because of the osmotic imbalance due to high salt and cold stress which may lead to physiological disorders.The stress-inducible proteins can directly protect against environmental conditions and regulate gene expression and signal transduction in response to stress. NCC have pivotal roles in osmotic adjustments, protection of cellular macromolecules, storage from of nitrogen, maintenance of cellular pH, detoxification of the cells, and scavenging of free radicals.Commercial experiences delivery of important traits in the field, including herbicide tolerance, pest resistance, modified wood properties, enhanced nitrogen metabolism, and male-sterility. However, a number of realities (challenges) have developed and are severely constraining further development. Harpin modulates genes expression involved in cell wall modifications, stress response, signal transduction, membrane transporting and photosynthesis system.

REFERENCES

Abdallah, Fathia, and Mohamed Chaieb. "Interactions of Acacia Raddiana with Herbaceous Vegetation Change with Intensity of Abiotic Stress." *Flora-Morphology, Distribution, Functional Ecology of Plants* 205.11 (2010): 738-744.

Araújo, A.P., M.G. Teixeira, and D.L. De Almeida. "Phosphorus Efficiency of Wild and Cultivated Genotypes of Common Bean (Phaseolus vulgaris L.) under Biological Nitrogen Fixation." *Soil Biology and Biochemistry* 29.5-6 (1997): 951-957.

Banowetz, Gary M., Mark D. Azevedo, and Richard Stout. "Morphological Adaptations of Hot Springs Panic Grass (Dichanthelium lanigunosum varsericeum (Schmoll) to Thermal Stress." *Journal of Thermal Biology* 33.2 (2008): 106-116.

Boschin, Giovanna, and Anna Arnoldi. "Legumes are Valuable Sources of tocopherols." *Food Chemistry* 127.3 (2011): 1199-1203.

Campos-Vega, Rocio, Guadalupe Loarca-Piña, and B. Dave Oomah. "Minor Components of Pulses and their Potential Impact on Human Health." *Food Research International* 43.2 (2010): 461-482.

Choi, Young-Jun, Francisco A. Tomás-Barberán, and Mikal E. Saltveit. "Wound-induced Phenolic Accumulation and Browning in Lettuce (Lactuca sativa L.) Leaf Tissue is Reduced by Exposure to n-alcohols." *Postharvest Biology and Technology* 37.1 (2005): 47-55.

Chuang, Huey-wen, *et al*. "A Harpin-induced Ethylene-responsive Factor Regulates Plant Growth and Responses to Biotic and Abiotic Stresses." *Biochemical and Biophysical Research Communications* 402.2 (2010): 414-420.

Doubnerová, Veronika, and Helena Ry lavá. "What can Enzymes of C4 Photosynthesis do for C3 Plants under Stress?." *Plant Science* 180.4 (2011): 575-583.

Edreva, Aglika. "Generation and Scavenging of Reactive Oxygen Species in Chloroplasts: A Submolecular Approach." *Agriculture, Ecosystems & Environment* 106. 2-3 (2005): 119-133.

Gorovits, Rena, and Henryk Czosnek. "Expression of Stress Gene Networks in Tomato Lines Susceptible and Resistant to Tomato Yellow Leaf Curl virus in Response to Abiotic Stresses." *Plant Physiology and Biochemistry* 46.4 (2008): 482-492.

Gregorio, G.B., *et al*. "Progress in Breeding for Salinity Tolerance and Associated Abiotic Stresses in Rice." *Field Crops Research* 76.2-3 (2002): 91-101.

Grover, Anil, *et al.* "Taming Abiotic Stresses in Plants through Genetic Engineering: Current Strategies and Perspective." *Plant Science* 143.1 (1999): 101-111.

Huang, Zhi, *et al.* "The Effects of Arbuscularmycorrhizal Fungi on Reactive Oxyradical Scavenging System of Tomato under Salt Tolerance." *Agricultural Sciences in China* 9.8 (2010): 1150-1159.

Kadioglu, Asim, *et al.* "Current Advances in the Investigation of Leaf Rolling caused by Biotic and Abiotic Stress Factors." *Plant Science* 182 (2012): 42-48.

Li, Qiao-Yun, *et al.* "Protective Role of Exogenous Nitric Oxide against Oxidative-stress Induced by Salt Stress in Barley (Hordeumvulgare)." *Colloids and Surfaces B: Biointerfaces* 65.2 (2008): 220-225.

Liang, Yongchao, *et al.* "Mechanisms of Silicon-mediated Alleviation of Abiotic Stresses in Higher Plants: A Review." *Environmental Pollution* 147.2 (2007): 422-428.

Lu, Xiao-Yan, and Xue-Lin Huang. "Plant miRNAs and Abiotic Stress Responses." *Biochemical and Biophysical Research Communications* 368.3 (2008): 458-462.

Parida, Asish Kumar, and Anath Bandhu Das. "Salt Tolerance and Salinity Effects on Plants: a Review." *Ecotoxicology and Environmental Safety* 60.3 (2005): 324-349.

Partridge, Mark, and Denis J. Murphy. "Roles of a Membrane-bound Caleosin and Putative Peroxygenase in Biotic and Abiotic Stress Responses in Arabidopsis." *Plant Physiology and Biochemistry* 47.9 (2009): 796-806.

Pasternak, Taras, *et al.* "Morphogenic Effects of Abiotic Stress: Reorientation of Growth in Arabidopsis Thaliana Seedlings." *Environmental and Experimental Botany* 53.3 (2005): 299-314.

Pernas, Mónica, Rosa Sánchez-Monge, and Gabriel Salcedo. "Biotic and Abiotic Stress can induce Cystatin Expression in Chestnut." *FEBS Letters* 467.2-3 (2000): 206-210.

Qados, Amira MS Abdul. "Effect of Salt Stress on Plant Growth and Metabolism of Bean Plant Viciafaba (L.)." *Journal of the Saudi Society of Agricultural Sciences* 10.1 (2011): 7-15.

Ranalli, P., and J. I. Cubero. "Bases for Genetic Improvement of Grain Legumes." *Field Crops Research* 53.1-3 (1997): 69-82.

Sano, Toshio, *et al.* "Calcium Ions are Involved in the Delay of Plant Cell Cycle Progression by Abiotic Stresses." *FEBS Letters* 580.2 (2006): 597-602.

Siddiqui, Manzer H., *et al.* "Nitrogen in Relation to Photosynthetic Capacity and Accumulation of Osmoprotectant and Nutrients in Brassica Genotypes Grown under Salt Stress." *Agricultural Sciences in China* 9.5 (2010): 671-680.

Sommer-Knudsen, Jens, Antony Bacic, and Adrienne E. Clarke. "Hydroxyproline-rich Plant Glycoproteins." *Phytochemistry* 47.4 (1998): 483-497.

Teixeira, Jorge, and Fernanda Fidalgo. "Salt Stress Affects Glutamine Synthetase Activity and mRNA Accumulation on Potato Plants in an Organ-dependent Manner." *Plant Physiology and Biochemistry* 47.9 (2009): 807-813.

Valdés-Rodríguez, Silvia, *et al.* "Cloning of a cDNA Encoding a Cystatin from Grain Amaranth (Amaranthus hypochondriacus) Showing a Tissue-specific Expression that is modified by Germination and Abiotic Stress." *Plant Physiology and Biochemistry* 45. 10-11 (2007): 790-798.

Vega, José M., *et al.* "Effect of Abiotic Stress on Photosynthesis and Respiration in Chlamydomonas reinhardtii: Induction of Oxidative Stress." *Enzyme and Microbial Technology* 40.1 (2006): 163-167.

Verslycke, Tim, and Colin R. Janssen. "Effects of a Changing Abiotic Environment on the Energy Metabolism in the Estuarine Mysid Shrimp Neomysis Integer (Crustacea: Mysidacea)." *Journal of Experimental Marine Biology and Ecology* 279.1-2 (2002): 61-72.

Wade, L.J. "Improving Tolerance to Abiotic Stresses in Rainfed Lowland Rice." *Field Crops Research* 2.76 (2002): 89-90.

Walsh, K.B. "Physiology of the Legume Nodule and its Response to Stress." *Soil Biology and Biochemistry* 27. 4-5 (1995): 637-655.

Zhang, Rui-Yue, *et al*. "Isolation and Expression Analysis of a Novel Abiotic Stress-induced Gene W89 from Wheat." *Agricultural Sciences in China* 6.4 (2007): 391-398.

Zhang, Zhen-Hua, *et al*. "Responses of Contrasting Rice (Oryza sativa L.) Genotypes to Salt Stress as Affected by Nutrient Concentrations." *Agricultural Sciences in China* 10.2 (2011): 195-206.

Section II: Sustainable Agriculture

Pages: 91-99

Irrigation Practices and Sustainable Agriculture
Edited by: **Dr. Prasann Kumar and Dr. Pawan Kumar 'Bharti'**
ISBN: 978-93-88854-31-3
Edition: **2020**
Published by: **Discovery Publishing House Pvt. Ltd., New Delhi (India)**

6 History of Agricultural Development

Prasann Kumar[1, 2*], Shipa Rani Dey[1]

GRAPHICAL ABSTRACT

Keywords: Agriculture, Biology, Development, History

INTRODUCTION

- Excavations, legends and remote sensing tests reveal that agriculture is 10,000 years old.
- Men concentrated on hunting and gathering (Paleolithic and Neolithic periods) during that time.

[1] Department of Agronomy, School of Agriculture, Lovely Professional University, Jalandhar - 144 411 (Punjab) (India)

[2] Divison of Research and Development, Lovely Professional University, Jalandhar - 144 411 (Punjab) (India)

- Women were the pioneers for cultivating useful plants from the wild flora.
- They dug out edible roots and rhizomes and buried the small ones for subsequent harvests.
- They used animal meat as main food and their skin for clothing.

EARLY DEVELOPMENT

1. The Bronze age (the early Aryans)

Period: 1800 to 1600 of BC

Aryans were depended on wheat, barley, millets, pulses, sesame, mustard & animal husbandry.

2. The Vedic age (1560-100 BC)

The profession of farming was regarded as only far the unlearned and those devoid of wisdom. It remained so far centuries.

3. The later Vedic period (1000-600BC)

Wooden ploughs were provided with iron ploughshares, their efficiency were further improved. This Improvement helped the Aryans to cultivate the virgin land resulted to greater mastery over food production.

4. The Buddhist period (Sixth century BC)

Brahmans were found pursuing village, cow herding, goat keeping, trade, woodwork, weaving, archery and carriage driving. The hired labour apparently was assigned a low social rank.

5. The Magadhan Empire (Fourth century BC)

Formations of villages started in this period. Plantation of bushes & tree, collection of seeds, fruit, flowers, fiber etc. started.

6. The Asoka Period

During this period, forestry and horticulture were promoted by encouraging plantation of trees in gardens and along roads in the farm of avenues.

7. First century BC to second century AD

First plough agriculture was introduced/developed to replace slash & burn cultivation. Knowledge of distant markets, origination of village settlements & breaded also some.

8. Age of the Guptas (300-500AD)

This period is called golden age of India. It provides information about agriculture besides other sciences. It deals with selection of land, manuring, cultivator, seed collection, sowing, planting & grafting. Amarasoka contains information on soil village &irrigation.

9. Empire of the Harshvardhana (606-647 AD)

The source of information on agriculture curling this period is writings of early Arab writers.

10. The Muslim Rule (1206-1761 AD)

During this period, land revenue system was improved. Taguai loans were given to cultivators in distressed circumstance for the purchase of seed & cattle.

The British Rule and Free India (1757-1947)

The historic developments in agriculture during British rules and free India

Year	Historic Developments
1871	Departments of Agriculture Created
1878	Higher Education in agriculture started at Coimbatore
1880	Famine Commission Appointed
1890	Higher Education Agriculture Started at Pune
1891	Dr. J.A. Voekker's Report on Improving Indian Agriculture Compiled
1900	Forest Research Institute (FRI) Established at Dehradun
1901	First Immigration Commission Constituted
1905	Imperial (Now Indian) Agricultural Research Institute Established at Pusa (Now at Delhi)
1921	Indian Central Cotton Committee Constituted
1926	Royal Commission on Agricultural Headed by Lord Linlithgow set up

Fig. 6.1: British rule & Free India
Source: based on review of literature

SOME IMPORTANT DEFINITIONS

History denotes the continuous record of past events.

Heritage indicates the inherited values carried from one generation to other generation.

Agricultural heritage denotes the values and traditional practices adopted in ancient India, which are more relevant for present day system.

AGRICULTURE HERITAGE IN INDIA

- Our heritage is unique than any other civilization.

- As a citizen of India, we must feel proud about our rich cultural heritage. Agriculture in India is not of recent origin, but has a long history dating back to Neolithic age of 7500-4000 B.C.
- It changed the life style of early man from nomadic hunter of wild berries and roots to cultivator of land.
- Agriculture is benefited from the wisdom and teachings of great saints. The wisdom gained and practices adopted have been passed down through generations.
- The traditional farmers have developed the nature friendly farming systems and practices such as mixed farming, mixed cropping, crop rotation etc.
- The great epics of ancient India convey the depth of knowledge possessed by the older generations of the farmers of India.

Important events in early history of Agriculture

Period	Name of Events
10000 BC	Hunting and Gathering
8700 BC	Domestication of Sheep
7500 BC	Wheat and Barley Cultivation
6000 BC	Domestication of Cattle's and Pigs
4400 BC	Maize Cultivation
3500 BC	Potato Cultivation
3400 BC	Wheel Invention
3000 BC	Bronze Tools
2900 BC	Plough Invention and Irrigation
2700 BC	Domestication of Silkworm in China
2300 BC	Cultivation of Chickpea, Pear and Sarson and Cotton
2200 BC	Domestication of Fowl, Buffalo and Elephant
2000 BC	Rice Cultivation
1800 BC	Finger-millet Cultivation
1725 BC	Sorghum Cultivation
1700 BC	Taming of Horse
1500 BC	Sugarcane Cultivation and Well Irrigation
1400 BC	Use of Iron
15th	Century Cultivation of Oranges, Brinjal
16th	Century Cultivation of Several Crops into India by Portuguese - Potato, Tomato, Chilies, Pumpkin, Papaya, Pineapple, Guava, Custard Apple, Groundnut, Tobacco, Cotton, Cashew nut

Fig. 6.2: Events in Early History of Agriculture

Source: based on review of literature

AGRICULTURE IN CIVILIZATION ERA

Indus valley civilization: In the year 1922, archaeologists dug up a few places in the Indus valley and carried out excavations at Mohenjodara (a mound of dead) in Sind (in Pakistan) and at Harappa on the river Ravi in Punjab. They observed that the people utilized the pots, utensils and ornaments. These cities were built along the river Indus and hence this civilization is known as Indus valley civilization. It is also known as Harappan culture and occupied the areas stretching from Delhi to Gujarat.

- During this period the people identified the importance of ploughing for the proper sowing of crop (i.e.) soil has to be stirred and seed has to be covered.
- Ox-drawn wheel cart was used for transport.
- The people cultivated wheat, barley, gram, peas, sesamum and rape.
- They also cultivated cotton and also devised methods of ginning, spinning and weaving.
- Animal husbandry was also given more importance during this period.
- They domesticated buffalo, cattle, camel, horse, elephant, and birds. They utilized them in agriculture and also for transport.
- **The Vedic civilization:** The word — Veda || is derived from — Vid || which means — Knowledge.
- Veda is the only literary source from which we know about the Aryans in India.

  Aryans were
- More prevalent during Vedic time which extends from Eastern Afghanistan, Kashmir, Punjab and Parts of Sind and Rajasthan. The land of Aryans was called land of seven rivers i.e., (Sutlej, Beas, Ravi, Chenab, Jhelum, Indus and Saraswathi). The Rig-Veda was the oldest book of Aryans.
- When they settled in the Punjab, they cut the jungles and built their villages.
- They grazed the animals in jungles and cultivated barley near the houses to protect from wild animals.
- Vedic people realized the importance of off-season ploughing and they started ploughing as and when the rain was received.
- Bullocks and ox were used for ploughing with regard to irrigation, channels were dug from the rivers.
- Wells were in use for supply of drinking water and irrigation called kucha wells, which were just holes dug in the ground. Even now such wells are in use in the river rain areas of northern India.

CIVILIZATIONS IN OTHER PARTS OF WORLD

- **Lemuria Civilization:** Lemuria was originally the name given to a vast hypothetical sunken continent or a land-bridge or landmass stretching from Ceylon to Madagascar all the way to the central Pacific Ocean across the Indian Ocean and Indonesia.
- Ancient Lemuria-map of India in 30,000 B.C.
- The lemurs derive their name from that of the Lemurs (or "Ancestors").Man descends from the apes.
- Hence, the name of Lemuria can be interpreted as "Land Ancestral" or "Land of the Ancestors".
- The ancient land tying India and Australia together that sank incrementally over time, is referred to as Lemuria.
- Farmers' status in the society during Indus, Vedic, Buddhist, Mauryan, Gupta and Sangam periods

Harappan period: The Indus Civilization had the first farming cultures in South Asia, which emerged in the hills of what is now called Baluchistan, to the west of the Indus Valley.

- The farmers took part in the so-called Neolithic Revolution, which took place in the Fertile Crescent around 9000 to 6000 BCE.
- These early farmers domesticated wheat and a variety of animals, including cattle.
- In the "Era" terminology, the Neolithic is known as the "Early Food Producing Era".

Vedic period: The most important people of the Vedic period are Vaishnava.

- There are four Vedic periods viz., Rig, Sama, Yajur, and Atharvana Vedas.
- In Rig Vedas period, the farmers occupied more number in the society. During this period, the superior people are called as Vaishnavas.
- The next position was Shathriyas and the least position occupied was Suthriyars.
- The Suthriyars are the farmers they cultivated the land and produced agricultural products under the land lord.
- The farmers status was more in AtharvaVedic period. They cultivated the crops based on the advice of the saints.

Buddhist period: A food producing economy emerged with the practice of agriculture on a wide scale by using iron implements.

- There was pleasant proprietorship in rural areas and there were no land lords.

- The village residents united undertook task such as laying irrigation channels, buildings, rest houses etc.
- The women extended their full co-operation in their works (public utility).
- Whole of each village was self-sufficient and life was simple.

Mauryan period: The economy was agrarian, majority of population were agriculturists.

- People were also engaged in animal husbandry and cattle rearing which meant additional income to peasants and the state.
- Gahapathi were the term used for head of rich land owing family.

Gupta period: The cultivators were called by various terms called Krishihala or Kinars.

- They had low social and economic life.

Sangam period: During Sangam literature, agriculture was the main occupation and hence the position of the farmers in the society was also high during this period.

- Agriculture Sangam was developed in Madurai.
- The farmers are called *uzhavar* (*plough man*) and also they are called as *Kalmar*.
- The land owners called *superior vellars* and the farmers who plough the land are called as inferior vellars.
- The farmers'status was mainly determined by the holding of land and animal population.

Thirukural period: Thiruvalluvar mentioned about importance of farmers in the society.

- In his statement — Farmers alone live an independent life.
- Others worship them and are second to them.
- If farmers stop cultivation, even Rishis (sages) cannot survive

CHRONOLOGICAL AGRICULTURAL TECHNOLOGY DEVELOPMENT IN INDIA

A. Early history (Before 1500 BCE)

1. **9000 BCE:** Wheat and barley were domesticated in the Indian sub-continent. This period also saw the first domestication of the elephant in addition of domestication of horse, sheep and goat.
2. **8000-6000 BCE:** Barley and wheat cultivation, along with the domestication of cattle, primarily sheep and goat was visible in Mehrgarh (Balochistan, now in Pakistan).Agro pastoralism in India included threshing, planting crops in rows - either of two or of six - and storing grain in granaries.

3. **5000 BCE:** Agricultural communities became widespread in Kashmir.
4. **5000-4000 BCE**: Cotton was cultivated. The Indus cotton industry was well developed and some methods used in cotton spinning and fabrication continued to be practiced till the modern Industrialization of India.
   - A variety of tropical fruit such as mango and muskmelon are native to the Indian sub-continent.
   - The Indians also domesticated hemp, which they used for a number of applications including making narcotics, fibre and oil.
   - The farmers of the Indus Valley grew peas, sesame, and dates.
   - Sugarcane was originally from tropical South Asia and Southeast Asia. Different species likely originated in different locations with S. barberi originating in India and S. edule and S. officinarum coming from New Guinea.
5. **5440 BCE:** Wild Oryza rice appeared in the Belan and Ganges valley regions of northern India. Rice was cultivated in the Indus Valley civilization.
6. **4500 BCE:** Irrigation was developed in the Indus Valley Civilization. The size and prosperity of the Indus civilization grew as a result of this innovation, which eventually led to more planned settlements making use of drainage.
7. **3000 BCE:** Sophisticated irrigation and water storage systems were developed by the Indus Valley civilization, including artificial reservoirs at Girnar.
   - **2600 BCE:** An early canal irrigation system from Circa.
   - **2500 BCE:** Archaeological evidence of an animal-drawn plough in the Indus Valley civilization.
   - **2000 BCE:** Agricultural activity included rice cultivation in the Kashmir and Harrappan regions.

CONCLUSION

At least eleven separate regions of the Old and New World were involved as independent centers of origin. Agriculture began independently in different parts of the globe, and included a diverse range of taxa. The history of agriculture records the domestication of plants and animals and the development and dissemination of techniques for raising them productively.

REFERENCES

https://en.wikipedia.org/wiki/History_of_agriculture

https://en.wikipedia.org/wiki/History_of_agriculture

https://www.newworldencyclopedia.org/entry/History_of_agriculture
https://www.crestcapital.com/tax/history_of_agriculture
https://www.environmentalscience.org/history-agriculture
https://www.monsantoglobal.com/...agriculture/.../a-brief-history-of-agriculture.aspx
https://www.britannica.com/topic/agriculture
https://www.encyclopedia.com/plants-and-animals/botany/botany.../history-agriculture
www.ecifm.rdg.ac.uk/history.htm
https://www.crystalinks.com/agriculturehistory.html

Pages: 100-113

Irrigation Practices and Sustainable Agriculture
Edited by: **Dr. Prasann Kumar and Dr. Pawan Kumar 'Bharti'**
ISBN: 978-93-88854-31-3
Edition: **2020**
Published by: **Discovery Publishing House Pvt. Ltd., New Delhi (India)**

7

Sustainable Agriculture for the Sustainable Life on Earth

Prasann Kumar[1, 2*], Johnson Yumnam[1]

GRAPHICAL ABSTRACT

Keywords: Agriculture, Development, Earth, Sustainable, Life

INTRODUCTION

The practice of farming using principles of ***ecology***, the study of relationships between organisms and their environment.

- *It has been defined as "an integrated system of plant and animal production practices having a site-specific application that will last over the long term:*

[1] Department of Agronomy, School of Agriculture, Lovely Professional University, Jalandhar - 144 411 (Punjab) (India)
[2] Divison of Research and Development, Lovely Professional University, Jalandhar - 144 411 (Punjab) (India)

- Satisfy human food and fiber needs
- Enhance environmental quality and the natural resource base upon which the agricultural economy depends
- Make the most efficient use of non-renewable resources and on-farm resources and integrate, where appropriate, natural biological cycles and controls
- Sustain the economic viability of farm operations
- Enhance the quality of life for farmers and society as a whole.

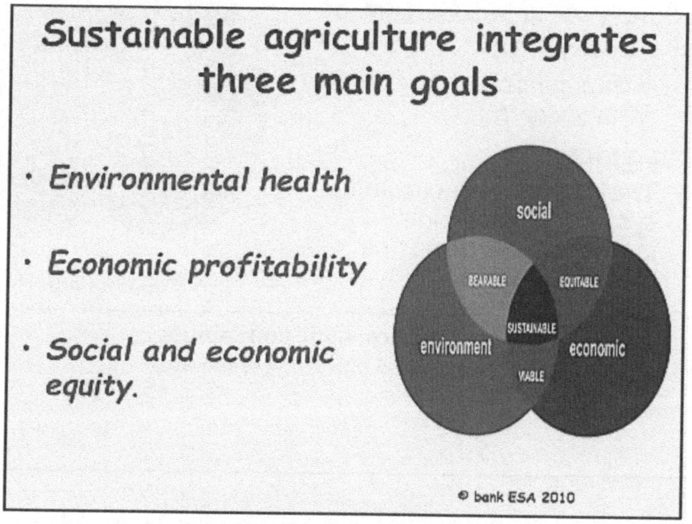

Fig. 7.1: Agriculture Integrates
Source: based on review of literature

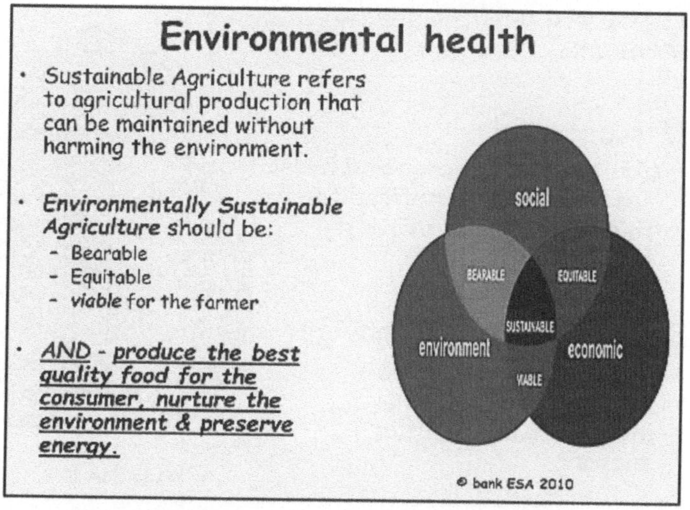

Fig. 7.2: Environmental health and agriculture
Source: based on review of literature

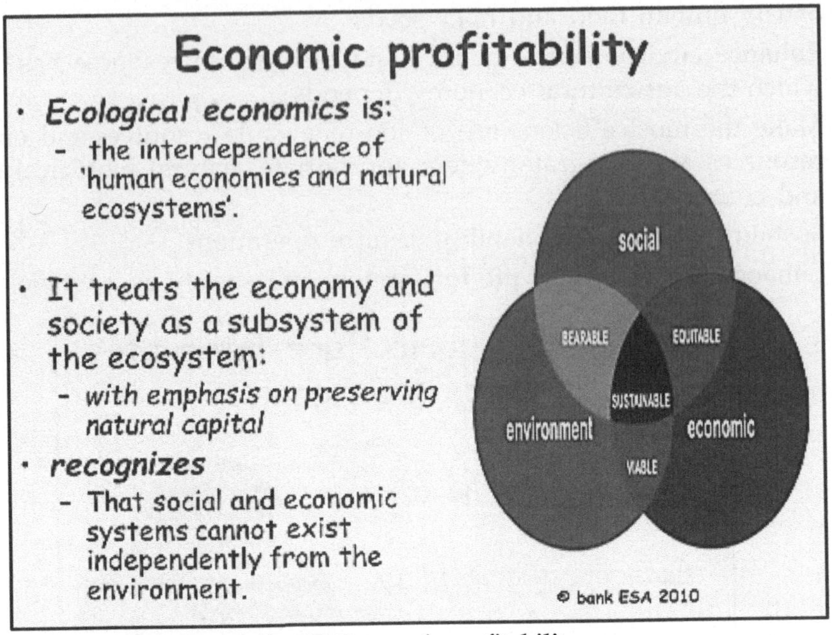

Fig. 7.3: Economic profitability
Source: based on review of literature

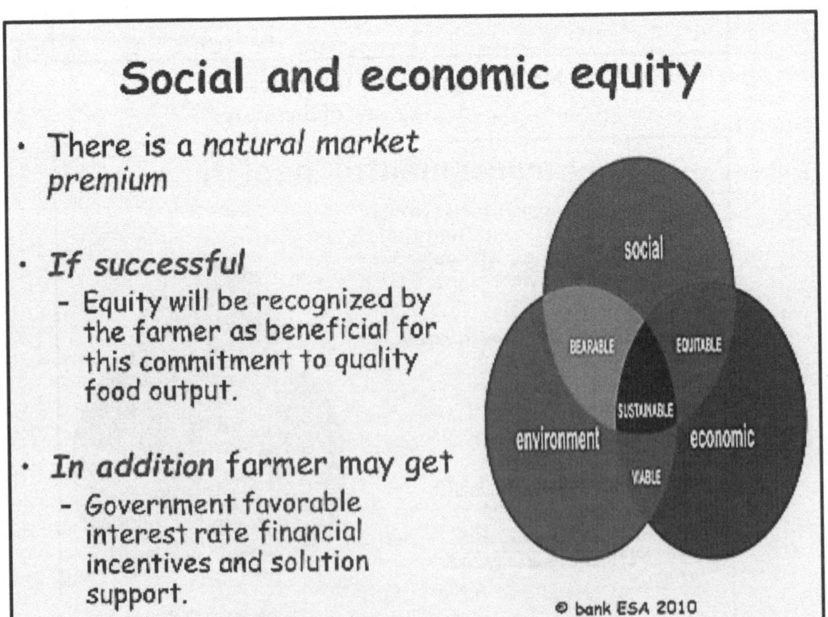

Fig. 7.4: Social and economic equity
Source: based on review of literature

SUSTAINABLE AGRICULTURE

- Sustainable agriculture in the United States was addressed by the 1990 farm bill.
- More recently, as consumer and retail demand for sustainable products has risen, organizations such as *Food Alliance* and *Protected Harvest* have started to provide measurement standards and certification programs for what constitutes a sustainable grown crop.

What is Sustainable Agriculture?

- Agriculture has changed dramatically, especially since the end of World War II.
- Food and fiber productivity soared due to new technologies, mechanization, increased chemical use, specialization and government policies that favored maximizing production.
- These changes allowed fewer farmers with reduced labor demands to produce the majority of the food and fiber in the U.S.
- Has had major social and ecological impacts, which have drawn intense praise and equally intense criticism.
- In fact, *many regions of the world peaked in food production in the period 1980 to 1995*
- Are presently in decline, *since desertification and critical water supplies have become limiting factors in a number of world regions.*
- Although these changes have had many positive effects and reduced many risks in farming, there have also been significant costs.

Prominent among these are:

- Topsoil depletion
- groundwater contamination
- decline of family farms
- continued neglect of the living and working conditions for farm laborers
- increasing costs of production
- Disintegration of economic and social conditions in rural communities.
- A growing movement has emerged during the past two decades to question the role of the agricultural establishment in promoting practices that contribute to these social problems.
- Today this movement for sustainable agriculture is garnering increasing support and acceptance within mainstream agriculture.
- Not only does sustainable agriculture address many environmental and social concerns, but it offers innovative and economically viable opportunities for growers, laborers, consumers, policymakers and many others in the entire food system.

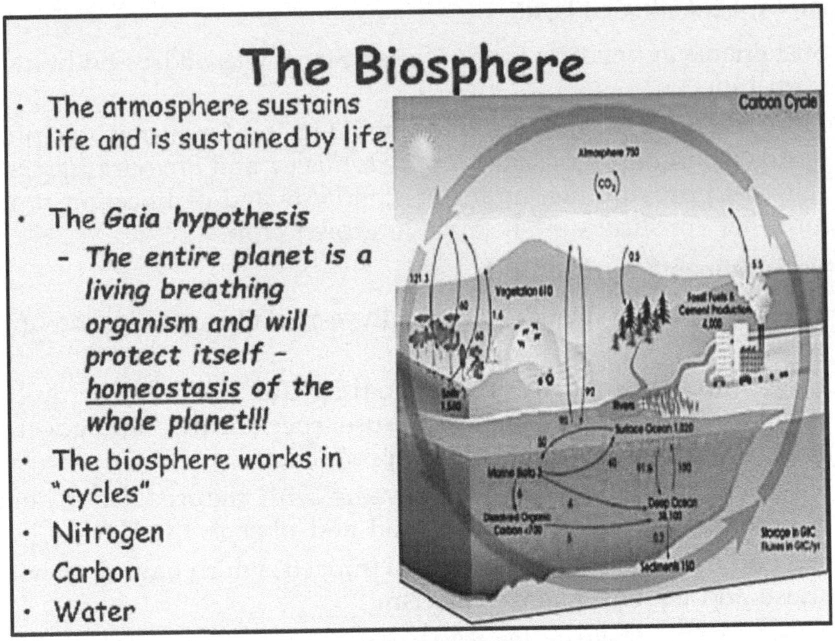

Fig. 7.5: The Biosphere

Source: based on review of literature

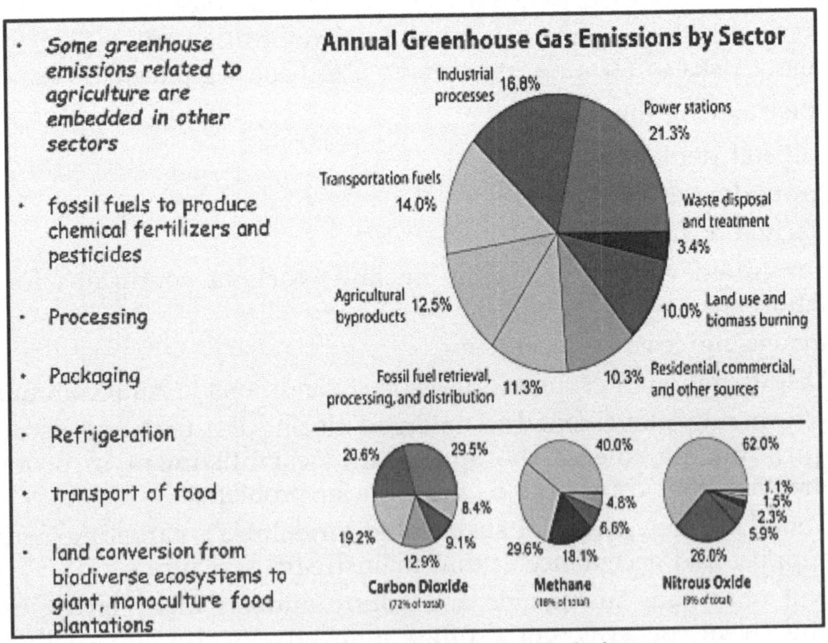

Fig. 7.6: Annual Greenhouse Gas Emissions

Source: based on review of literature

RODALE INSTITUTE STUDY

- projects that the planet's *3.5 billion tillable acres* could sequester nearly *40 percent of current CO_2 emissions* if they were converted to "regenerative" organic agriculture practices.
- *Remember:*
- Via photosynthesis, over 100 billion metric tons of CO_2 and H_2O are converted into cellulose and other plant products

MANY STUDIES HAVE DRAWN SIMILAR CONCLUSION

- ***India***
  - Organic farming research shows *increases in carbon absorption by up to 55 percent* (even higher when agro-forestry is added into the mix), and water holding capacity is increased by *10 percent*.
- ***California***
  - Study of 20 commercial farms found that organic fields had *28 percent more carbon in the soil* than industrial farms.

WATER

- In some areas, sufficient rainfall is available for crop growth, but many other areas require irrigation.
- For irrigation systems to be sustainable they require proper management (*to avoid salinization*) and must not use more water from their source than is naturally replenished.

INDICATORS FOR SUSTAINABLE WATER RESOURCE DEVELOPMENT ARE:

- Internal renewable water resources.
  - This is the average annual flow of rivers and groundwater generated from endogenous precipitation.
  - Can be expressed in three different units:
  - in absolute terms (km^3/yr)
  - a measure of the humidity of the country (mm/yr)
  - As a function of population (m^3/person per yr).
- Global renewable water resources.
  - Sum of internal renewable water resources and incoming flow originating outside the country.
  - Can vary with time if upstream development reduces water availability at the border.

INDICATORS FOR SUSTAINABLE WATER RESOURCE DEVELOPMENT ARE:

- **Dependency ratio**
  - This is the proportion of the global renewable water resources originating outside the country, expressed in percentage.

  - It is an expression of the level to which the water resources of a country depend on neighboring countries.
- **Water withdrawal**
  - When expressed in percentage of water resources, it shows the degree of pressure on water resources.
  - A rough estimate shows that if water withdrawal exceeds a quarter of global renewable water resources of a country, water can be considered a limiting factor to development.
  - Therefore, the pressure on water resources can have a direct impact on all sectors, from agriculture to environment and fisheries.

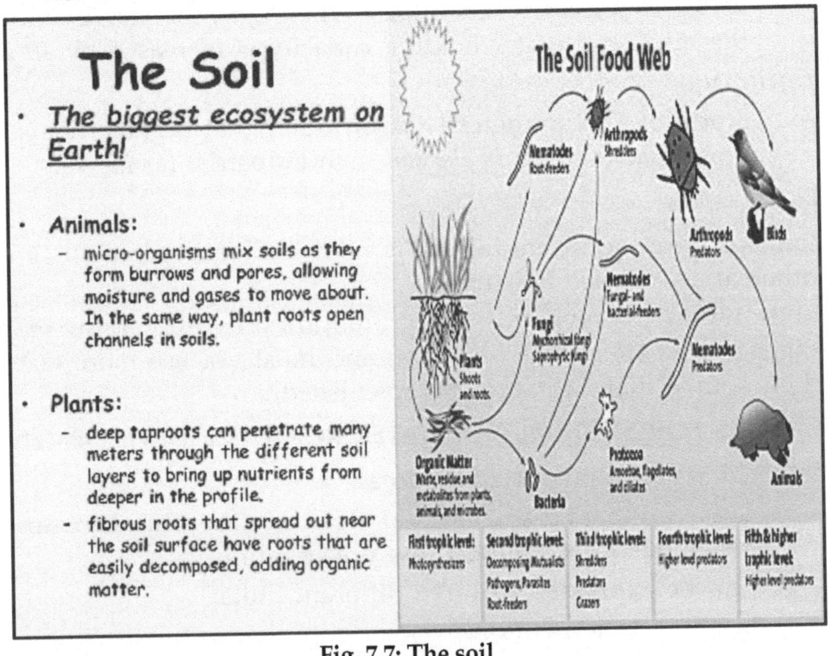

Fig. 7.7: The soil

Source: based on review of literature

SOIL EROSION

- Fast becoming one of theworlds greatest problems. It is estimated that more than a thousand million tonnes of southern Africa's soil are eroded every year.
  - Experts predict that crop yields will be halved within thirty to fifty years if erosion continues at present rates.
- **Not unique to Africa but is occurring worldwide.**
  - The phenomenon is being called *Peak Soil* as present large scale factory farming techniques are jeopardizing humanity's ability to grow food in the present and in the future.

- Without efforts to improve soil management practices, the availability of arable soil will become increasingly problematic.

SOIL MANAGEMENT TECHNIQUES

- No-till farming
  - Soil is left intact and crop residue is left on the field.
  - Soil layers, conserving organisms and layers in their natural state.
- Keyline design
  - Maximizes beneficial use of water resources of a piece of land.
  - Refers to a specific topographic feature linked to water flow
- Growing wind breaks to hold the soil
  - Planting trees and hedges
  - Prevent wind from blowing away top soil
- Incorporating organic matter back into fields
  - Composting! Puts Carbon, Nitrogen, Oxygen, Water and microbes back into the soil!!! Can also add Urine –honest!!
- Stop using chemical fertilizers (contain salt)
  - Remember Algal Blooms? Also, the salt kills natural micro-organisms in soil – contaminates water!!!!!
- Protecting soil from water runoff
  - Careful placement of rocks and trees.
- Soil Steaming
  - sterilize soil with steam in open fields or greenhouses
  - Destroys pathogens
  - Destroys weeds, but dead plant material is left in soil as compost

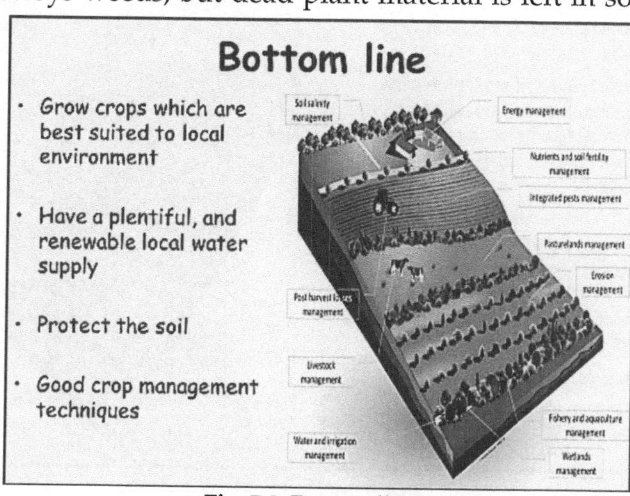

Fig. 7.8: Bottom line

Source: based on review of literature

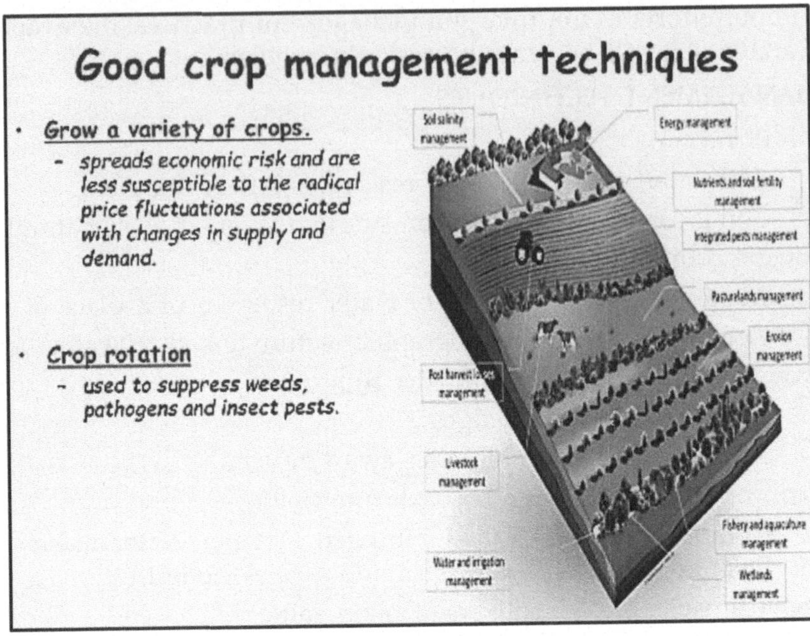

Fig. 7.9: Crop management

Source: based on review of literature

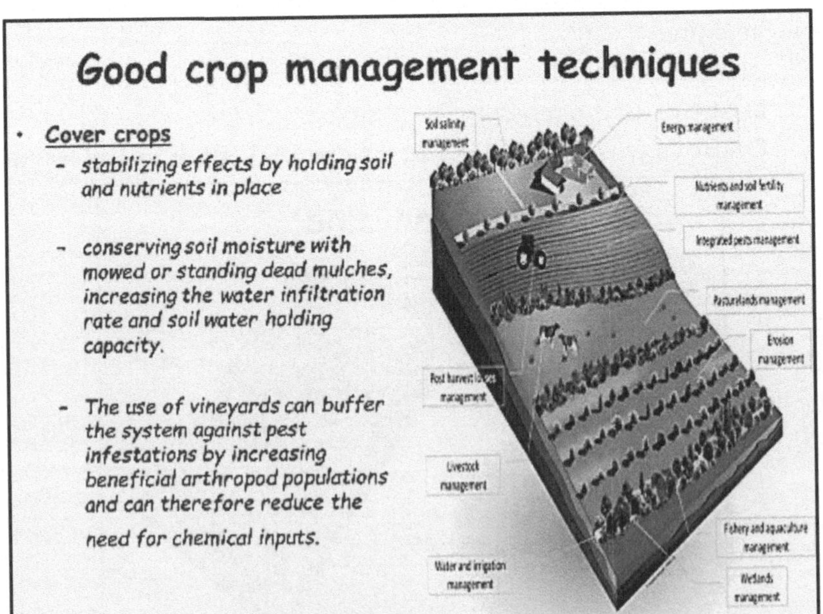

Fig. 7.10: Cover crops

Source: based on review of literature

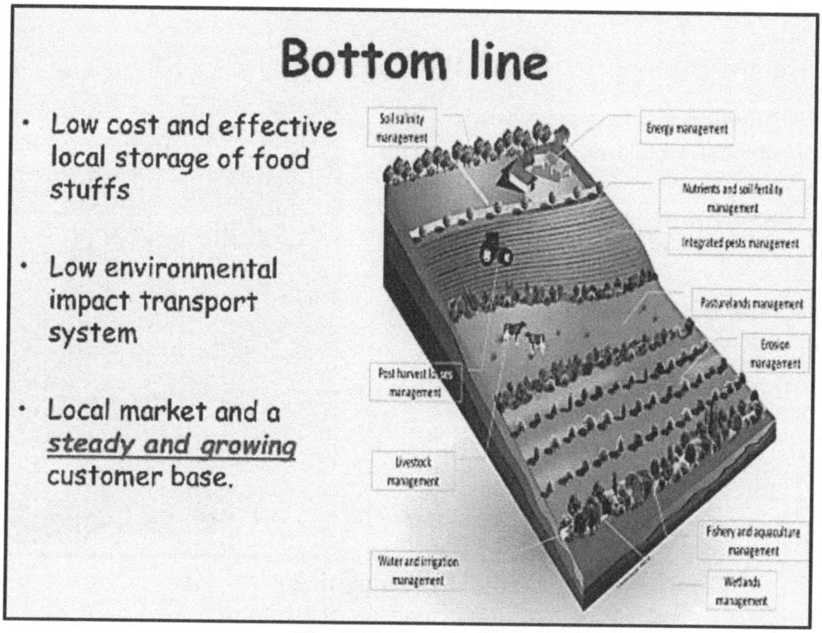

Fig. 7.11: Bottom line

Source: based on review of literature

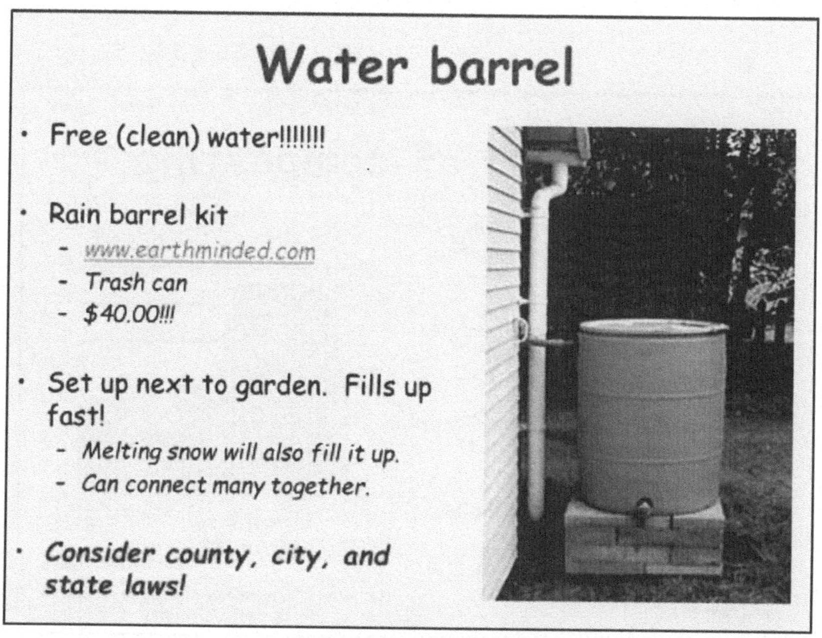

Fig. 7.12: Water barrel

Source: based on review of literature

Fig. 7.13: Composting
Source: based on review of literature

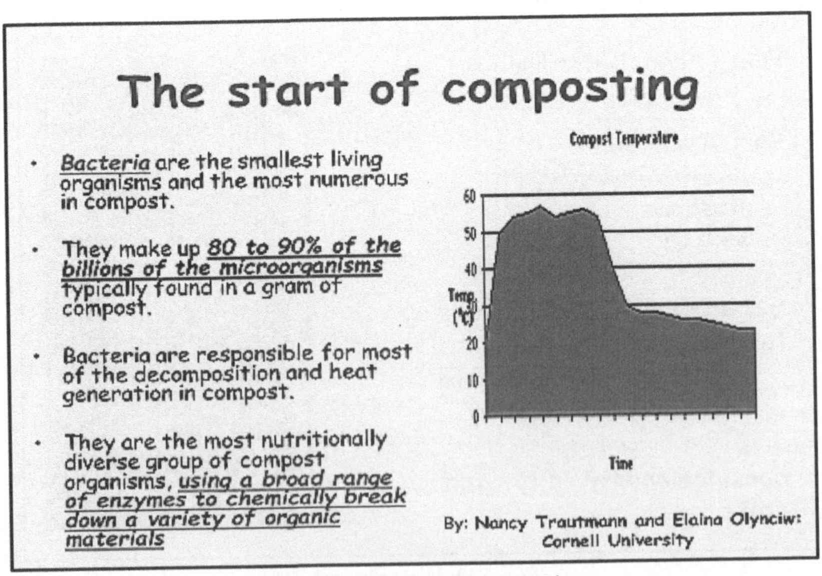

Fig. 7.14: Onset of composting
Source: based on review of literature

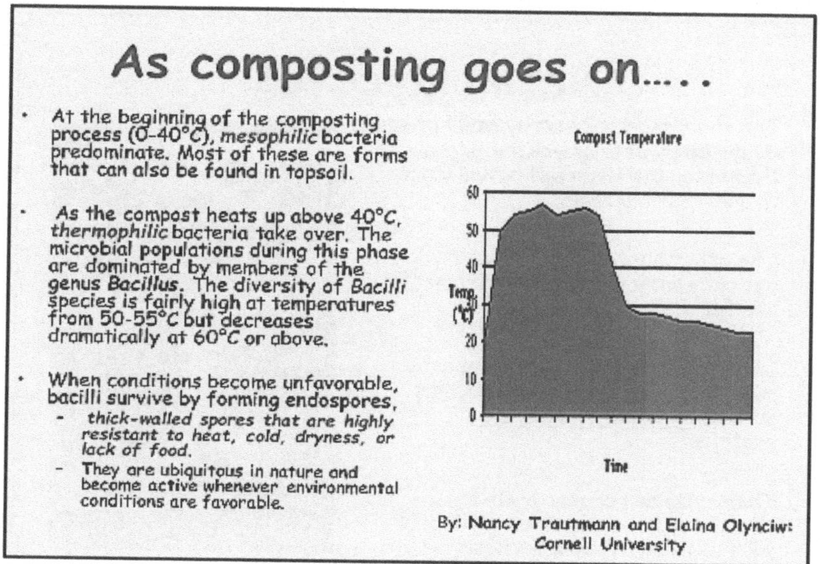

Fig. 7.15: Ongoing composting

Source: based on review of literature

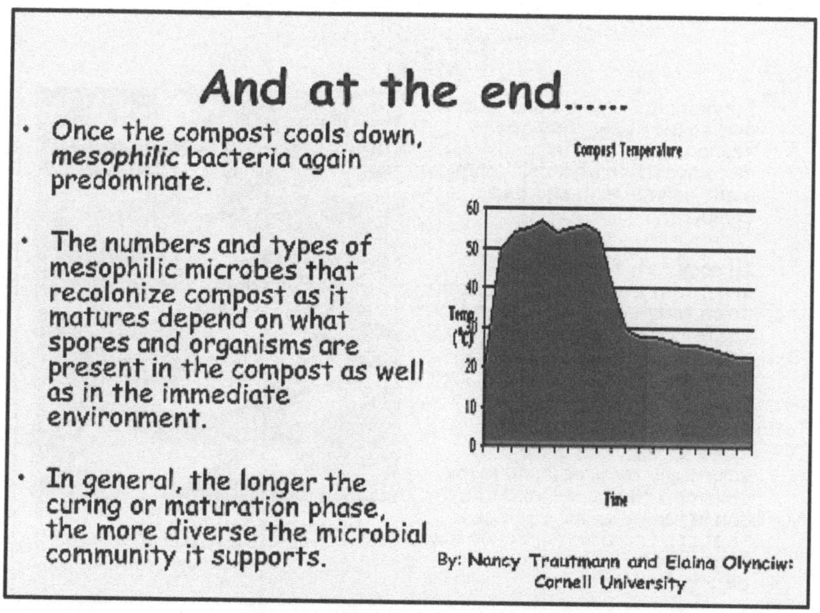

Fig. 7.16: End of the composting

Source: based on review of literature

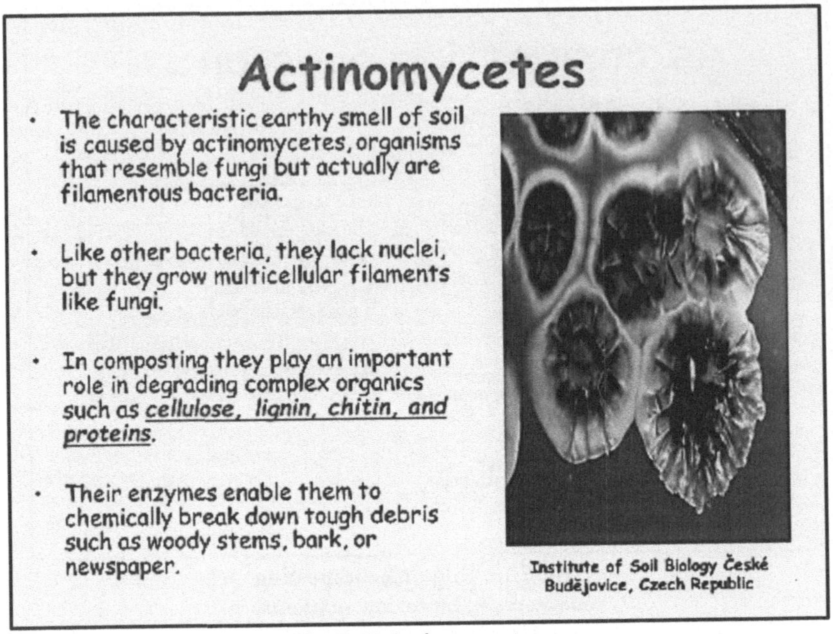

Fig. 7.17: Actinomycetes

Source: based on review of literature

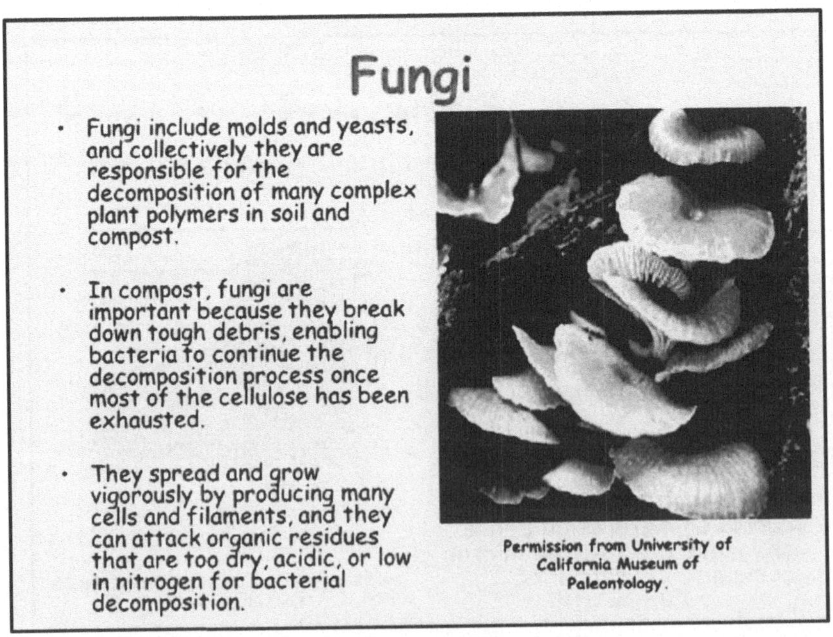

Fig. 7.18: Fungi

Source: based on review of literature

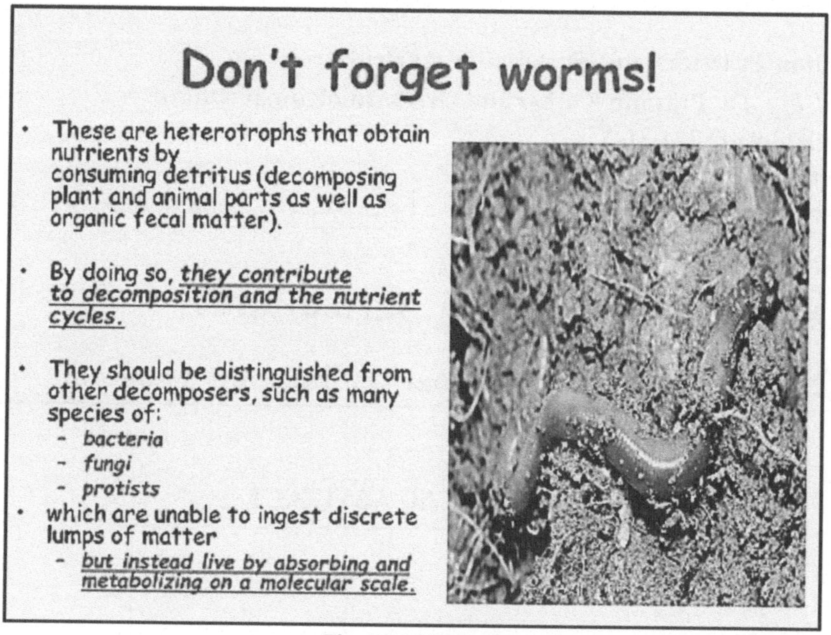

Fig. 7.19: Worms

Source: based on review of literature

So what about *backyard* Agricultural Sustainability?

- Grow *only* crops which mature within the local growing season.
- Only grow crops selections which will work together in such a limited space.
- Think about nutrient needs.
- Think about water demands.
- Think about long time storage of successful crops.

CONCLUSION

- Converts raw organic matter into humus, feeds the soil population of microorganisms and other creatures, thus maintains high and healthy levels of soil life.
- Decomposition of dead plant material causes complex organic compounds to be slowly oxidized or to break down into simpler forms which are further transformed into microbial biomass.
- The biochemical structure of humus enables it to moderate – or buffer – excessive acid or alkaline soil conditions.
- The dark color of humus (usually black or dark brown) helps to warm up cold soils in the spring.

Pages: 114-123

Irrigation Practices and Sustainable Agriculture
Edited by: Dr. Prasann Kumar and Dr. Pawan Kumar 'Bharti'
ISBN: 978-93-88854-31-3
Edition: 2020
Published by: Discovery Publishing House Pvt. Ltd., New Delhi (India)

8 Why Agriculture?

Prasann Kumar[1, 2*], Johnson Yumnam[1]

GRAPHICAL ABSTRACT

Keywords: Agriculture, Crops, Plant, Scope

INTRODUCTION

Agriculture

Latin word Ager or Agri meaning soils &cultura means cultivation. Cultivation/production of crop plants or livestock products.

[1] Department of Agronomy, School of Agriculture, Lovely Professional University, Jalandhar - 144 411 (Punjab) (India)
[2] Divison of Research and Development, Lovely Professional University, Jalandhar - 144411 (Punjab) (India)

Agronomy

Greek words agros meaning field and nomos means to manage.

Branch of Agricultural Science dealing with the principles and practices of crop production.

AGRICULTURE AS ART

- Way to perform the operation of a farm in a skillful manner.
- Physical and mental skills are involved in agriculture.
- Ploughing, handling animals, sowing, transplanting.
- Mental skills are those involved in decision making.

AGRICULTURE AS SCIENCE

- Scientific principles are employed
- The scientific principles of various branches
- Based on general laws and principles.

AGRICULTURE IS A BUSINESS

- Intended to earn more income.
- Demands business knowledge
- Land, labour, capital are judiciously used.
- Tailors the production with demand to earn more profits.
- Agricultural Engineering - It is an important component for crop production and horticulture particularly to provide tools and implements. It is aiming to produce modified tools to facilitate proper animal husbandry and crop production tools, implements and machinery in animal production.
- Forestry - It deals with production of large scale cultivation of perennial trees for supplying wood, timber, rubber, etc. and also raw materials for industries.
- Fishery Science - It is for marine fish and inland fishes including shrimps and prawns.

GREEN REVOLUTION

Term first used in 1968 by former USAID Director William Gaud said

- Use of High-yielding variety seeds
- Increased use of chemical fertilizers
- Irrigation

WHICH RESULTED INTO

- The increase in production
- Made India self-sufficient in food grains
- Improved condition of agriculture in India

- High-yielding wheat was first introduced to India in 1968 by American agronomist Norman Borlaug.
- Hailed as the Father of the Green Revolution because he introduced "Norin 10", a Japanese dwarf variety of wheat
- M.S. Swaminathan is known as the "Father of the Green Revolution in India".
- Use of high yielding varieties (HYV) of seeds.

A. Crop Improvement	*(i)* Plant breeding and genetics *(ii)* Bio-technology
B. Crop Management	*(i)* Agronomy *(ii)* Social Science and Agricultural Chemistry *(iii)* Seed Technology *(iv)* Agricultural Microbiology *(v)* Crop-Physiology *(vi)* Agricultural Engineering *(vii)* Environmental Sciences *(viii)* Agricultural Meteorology
C. Crop Protection	*(i)* Agricultural Entomology *(ii)* Plant Pathology *(iii)* Nematology
D. Social Sciences	*(i)* Agricultural Extension *(ii)* Agricultural Economics
Allied disciplines	*(i)* Agricultural Statistics *(ii)* English and Tamil *(iii)* Mathematics *(iv)* Bio-Chemistry etc.

Fig. 8.1: Scope of agriculture
Source: based on review of literature

Fig. 8.2: Forms of agriculture
Source: based on review of literature

MEASURES ADOPTED IN GREEN REVOLUTION

- Use of high yielding varieties (HYV) of seeds
- Irrigation
- Use of insecticides and pesticides
- Consolidation of holdings
- Land reforms
- Improved rural infrastructure
- Supply of agricultural credit
- Use of (chemical) fertilizers
- Use of Sprinklers or Drip Irrigation

IMPACTS OF GREEN REVOLUTION

Positive Impacts

- Increase in production/yield.
- Advantage to farmers
  - economic situation
  - getting better yield
  - Pests control
  - Mechanization
  - Better land use
- Better scientific methods
- New seeds have been developedcountry's economic development

Negative Impacts

- Degradation of land
  - Land quality
  - Carbon material has gone down.
- Weeds have increased
- Pest infestation has gone up
- Loss of Bio Diversity
- Contamination of ground water.
- Soil infertile.
- Affect human's health.

How Green Revolution help to remove Flaws of Agriculture

- Low Irrigation Facility
- Frequent Occurrence of Famines
- Lack of Finance (credit)

SELF-SUFFICIENCY

- Marketing Agriculture
- What is Agronomy?
- Greek words "AGRO" meaning field & "NOMO" meaning to manage.

DEFINITION OF AGRONOMY

1. Agronomy is branch of agril science which deals with principles and practices of soil, water and crop management.
2. It is branch of agril science that deals with methods which providefavorable environment to the crop for higher productively
3. It deals with the study of principles and preaches of crop production and field management.
4. It is the study of planet in relation to soil and climate. It deals essentially with all aspects of soil, crop and water management to increase productively of crops.

SCOPE OF AGRONOMY

- Agronomy is a dynamic discipline
- Practices and modified of new practices developed for high productively as follows:
    1. Proper methods of filling the lands.
    2. Suitable period for its cultivation.
    3. Farm implements in good shape and managing field crops.
    4. Management of crops, livestock& their feedings.
    5. Care and disposal of farm & animal products.
    6. Proper maintenance of accounts
    7. Availability of chemical fertilizers has necessitated the generation of knowledge on the method.
    8. A vast knowledge about selectivity, time and method of herbicides application.
    9. Water management practices.
    10. Intensive cropping.
    11. New technology to overcome the effect of moisture stress under dry land condition.
    12. Packages of practices to explore full potential of new varieties of crops.

PRINCIPLES OF AGRONOMY

"Principles of agronomy deals with basic concepts and common agronomic principles and much more than crop to crop management approaches"

- Agro-meterology
- Soils and Tillage
- Soils and Water conservation
- Dry land Agriculture:
- Mineral Nutrition of plants, Manures and Fertilizers
- Irrigation and water management
- Weed Management
- Cropping and Farming systems.
- Sustainable Agriculture.

RELATIONSHIP OF AGRONOMY WITH OTHER SCIENCES

Agronomy is having Relationship with both basic and Applied Sciences

- **Basic sciences** are those which reveal the facts or secrets of natureand comprise subjects like chemistry, physics, math's, botany, zoology
- **Applied sciences** are those in which the theories and lawspropounded in basic sciences are applied to problems in agriculture and other fields.
- Agronomy is essentially an applied science

Classifications of Cropping System based on Intensity of Cultivation

Mono-cropping or Single Cropping: growing only one crop on a particular land year after year. e.g.

- Groundnut or cotton or sorghum
- Flue-cured tobacco is grown in Güntur (A.P.)
- Rice crop is grown
- **Monoculture:** Practice of repetitive growing only crop irrespective of its intensity as rice-rice-rice in Kerala, West Bengal and Orissa.
- **Sole Cropping:** One crop variety grown alone in pure stand at normal density.

AS A SCIENCE

- It utilizes all modern technologies developed on scientific principles such as:
  - Crop improvement/breeding
  - Crop production
  - Crop protection
  - Economics etc.

AS THE BUSINESS

- As long as agriculture is the way of life of the rural population, production is ultimately bound to consumption. But agriculture as a business aims at maximum net return through.

- The management of land, labour, water and capital
- Employing the knowledge of various sciences for production of food, feed, fibre and fuel.

Different agents who make up the food chain are:

- Producers
- Transporters
- Processors
- Wholesalers
- Retailers
- Consumers

All are linked by a series of physical and financial flows.Physical level of food production determined by:

- area planted;
- soil fertility and climate;
- technology available; and
- use of inputs such.

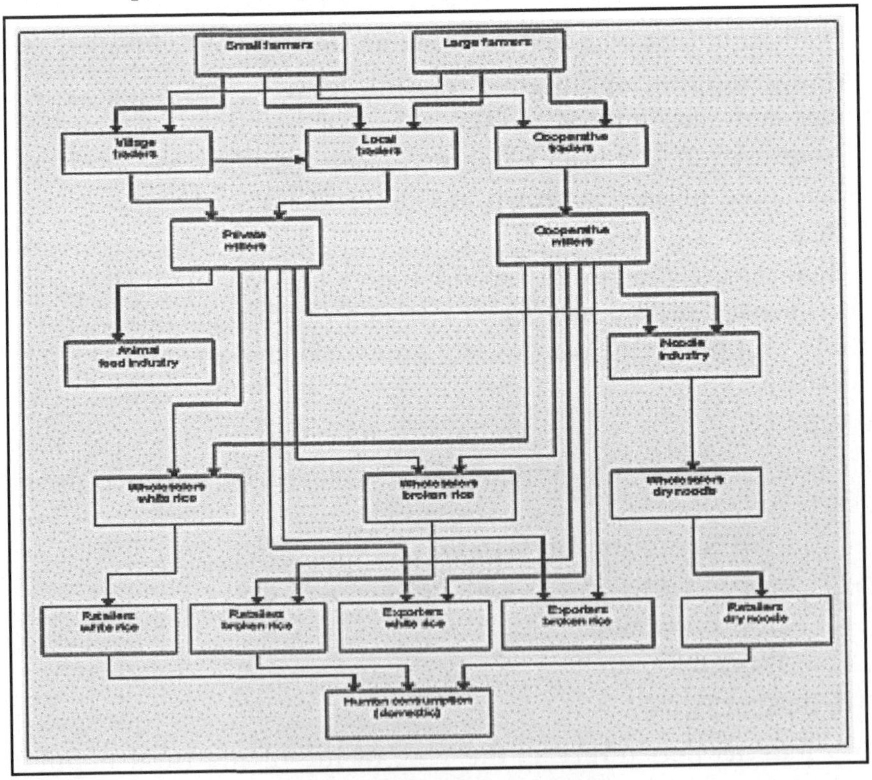

Fig. 8.3: Cross talks of practices

Source: Based on review of literature

IMPORTANT EVENTS IN THE HISTORY OF AGRICULTURE

Period	Events
• 10,000 BC	Hunting and gathering
• 7500 BC	Invention of polished stone implements and Wheat and Barley cultivation in middle east
• 4400 BC	Maize was cultivated in Mexico
• 3500 BC	Potato was grown in south America
• 2900 BC	Plough was used in middle east and irrigation
• 2700 BC	Silk moth was domesticated in China
• 2000 BC	Rice cultivation started in India
• 1725 BC	Jowar (Sorghum) cultivation started in Rajasthan
• 1000-1600 BC	Iron ploughs were in use

DEVELOPMENT OF SCIENTIFIC AGRICULTURE IN WORLD

1. Francis Bacon (1561-1624 A.D.): Found the water as nutrient of plants
2. G.R. Glanber (1604-1668 A.D.): Salt peter (KNO_3) as nutrient and not water
3. Jethrotull (1674-1741 A.D.): Fine soil particle as plant nutrient
4. Priestly (1730-1799 A.D.): Discovered the oxygen
5. Thomas Jefferson (1793 A.D.): Developed the mould board plough.
6. Theodore-de-Saussure: Found that plants absorb CO_2 from air and release O2; soil supply N_2 and ash to plants.
7. Justus van Liebig (1804-1873 A.D.): A German chemist developed the concept called "Liebig's law of minimum".

It states as follows. "A deficiency or absence of the necessary constituent, all others being present, renders the soil barren for crops for which that nutrient is needed"–It is referred as "Barrel concept".

E.A. Mitsherlich (1909) proposed a theory of "Law of diminishing returns" states that, 'The increase in any crop produce by a unit increment of a deficient factor is proportional to the decrement of that factor from the maximum and the response is curvilinear instead of linear.Mitscherlich equation is $dy/dx = C\ (A\text{-}Y)$. *Wilcox* (1929) proposed "Inverse Yield–Nitrogen law" states that, the growth and yielding ability of any crop plant is inversely proportional to the mean nitrogen content in the dry matter".

A. **Shifting Cultivationor aka Assartage system**
B. **Subsidiary Farming-**cultivation, gathering and hunting
C. **Subsistence Farming-**"Grow it and eat it"
D. **Mixed Farming-**Field crop-grass husbandry

E. **Advanced Farming**
   - selection of crops and varieties, pasture management,

F. **Scientific Agriculture (19th Century)**
   - Agriculture took the shape of a teaching science.

G. **Present Day Agriculture (21st Century)**
   - A business like livestock (dairy), poultry, fishery, piggery, sericulture, apiary, plantation cropping etc.

MEASURES ADOPTED IN GREEN REVOLUTION

- Use of high yielding varieties (HYV) of seeds
- Irrigation
- Use of insecticides and pesticides
- Consolidation of holdings
- Land reforms
- Improved rural infrastructure
- Supply of agricultural credit
- Use of (chemical) fertilizers
- Use of Sprinklers or Drip Irrigation

IMPACTS OF GREEN REVOLUTION

Positive Impacts

- Increase in production/yield.
- Advantage to farmers
  - economic situation
  - getting better yield
  - Pests control
  - Mechanization
  - Better land use
- Better scientific methods
- New seeds have been developed
- Country's economic development

Negative Impacts

- Degradation of land
  - Land quality
  - Carbon material has gone down
- Weeds have increased
- Pest infestation has gone up
- Loss of Bio Diversity

- Contamination of ground water
- Soil infertile.
- Affect human's health

How green revolution help to remove flaws of agriculture

- Low Irrigation Facility
- Frequent Occurrence of Famines
- Lack of Finance (credit)
- Self-sufficiency
- Marketing Agriculture

CONCLUSION

The history of agriculture began thousands of years ago.Plants were independently cultivated in at least 11 regions of the world. Industrial agriculture based on large-scale monoculture in the twentieth century came to dominate agricultural output, though about 2 billion people still depended on subsistence agriculture into the twenty-first.Agriculture is the science and art of cultivating plants and livestock. Agriculture was the key development in the rise of sedentary human civilization, whereby farming of domesticated species created food surpluses that enabled people to live in cities.After gathering wild grains beginning at least 105,000 years ago, nascent farmers began to plant them around 11,500 years ago. Pigs, sheep and cattle were domesticated over 10,000 years ago.

REFERENCES

https://www.sciencedaily.com/terms/agriculture.htm
agricoop.nic.in/
https://www.sciencedaily.com/terms/agriculture.htm
https://www.downtoearth.org.in/agriculture
https://www.india.gov.in/topics/agriculture
agritech.tnau.ac.in/agriculture/agri_index.html
Vikaspedia.in/agriculture
www.fao.org/e-agriculture/
https://dbtagriculture.bihar.gov.in/
https://www.newworldencyclopedia.org/entry/Agriculture

Pages: 124-133

Irrigation Practices and Sustainable Agriculture
Edited by: **Dr. Prasann Kumar and Dr. Pawan Kumar 'Bharti'**
ISBN: 978-93-88854-31-3
Edition: **2020**
Published by: **Discovery Publishing House Pvt. Ltd., New Delhi (India)**

9 Green Revolution

Prasann Kumar[1,2*], Johnson Yumnam[1]

GRAPHICAL ABSTRACT

Keywords: Agriculture, Biotic, Green, Revolution

INTRODUCTION

The green revolution is the significant increase in agricultural productivity resulting from the introduction of high - yield varieties of grains, use of pesticides, and improved management techniques.

[1] Department of Agronomy, School of Agriculture, Lovely Professional University, Jalandhar - 144 411 (Punjab) (India)
[2] Divison of Research and Development, Lovely Professional University, Jalandhar - 144 411 (Punjab) (India)

Fig. 9.1: Founder of green revolution along with Smt. Indira Gandhi
Source: based on review of literature

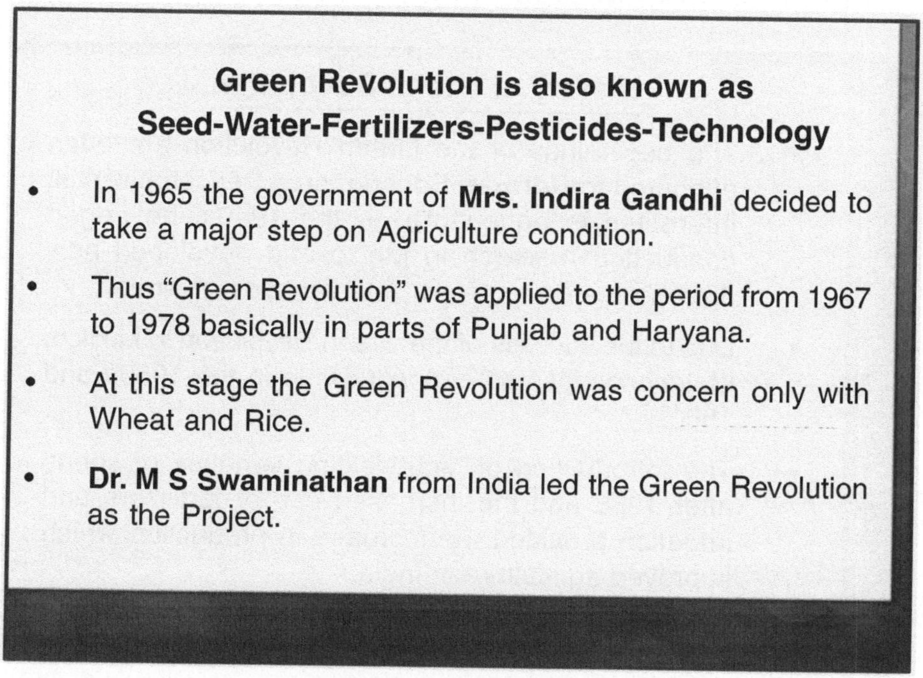

Fig. 9.2: Green revolution
Source: based on review of literature

Fig. 9.3: Green revolution output
Source: based on review of literature

History of Green Revolution

- The beginnings of the Green Revolution are often attributed to **Norman** Borlaug, an American scientist interested in agriculture. In the 1940s, he began conducting research in Meixo and developed new disease resistance high-yield varieties of wheat.
- Due to the success of the Green Revolution in Mexico, its technologies spread worldwide in the 1950s and 1960s.
- The introduction of high-yielding varieties of seeds after 1965 and the increased use of fertilizers and irrigation provided the increase in production which improved agriculture in India.

Fig. 9.4: History of Green Revolution
Source: based on review of literature

Methods Used in Green Revolution

- Double/Multiple Cropping system
- Seeds with superior genetics
- Proper irrigation system
- High Yielding Variety (HYV) of seeds
- Use of pesticides and fertilizers
- Use of modern machinery (Tractor, Harvested, Thrasher)
- Expansion of farming areas

Fig. 9.5: Methods used in green revolution
Source: based on review of literature

Basic Elements in Green Revolution

- **Continued expansion of farming areas:**
  Green Revolution continued with quantitative expansion of farmlands.
- **Double-cropping existing farmland:**
  Instead of one crop season per year, the decision was made to have two crop seasons per year.
  There had to be two "monsoons" per year. One would be the natural 'monsoon' and the other an artificial 'monsoon'.
- **Using seeds with superior genetics:**
  This was the scientific aspect of the Green Revolution to use High Yielding Variety (HYV) of seeds.

Fig. 9.6: Elements in green revolution
Source: based on review of literature

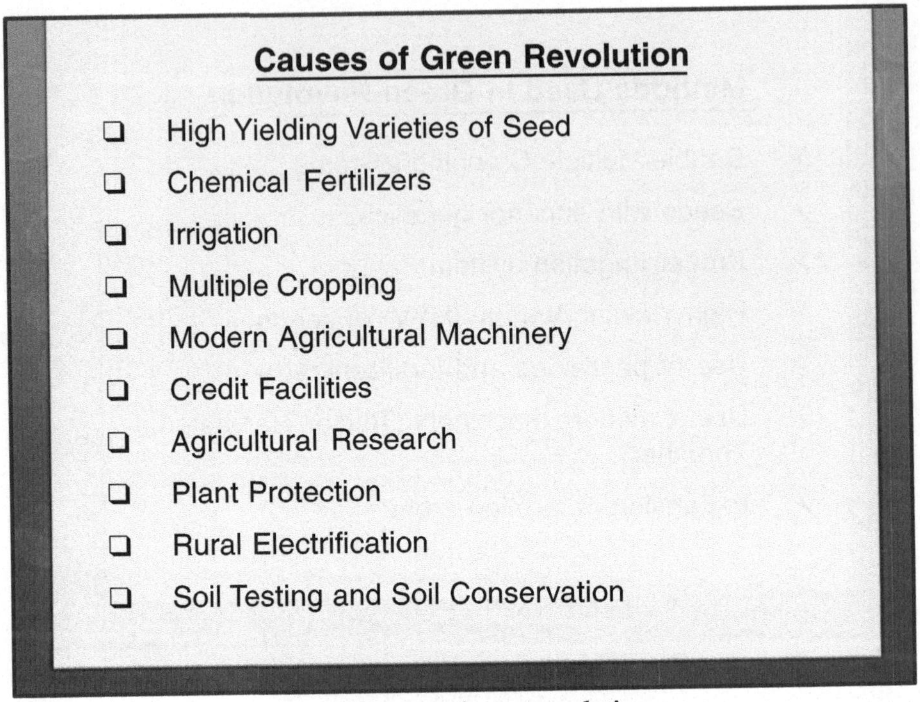

Fig. 9.7: Causes of green revolution
Source: based on review of literature

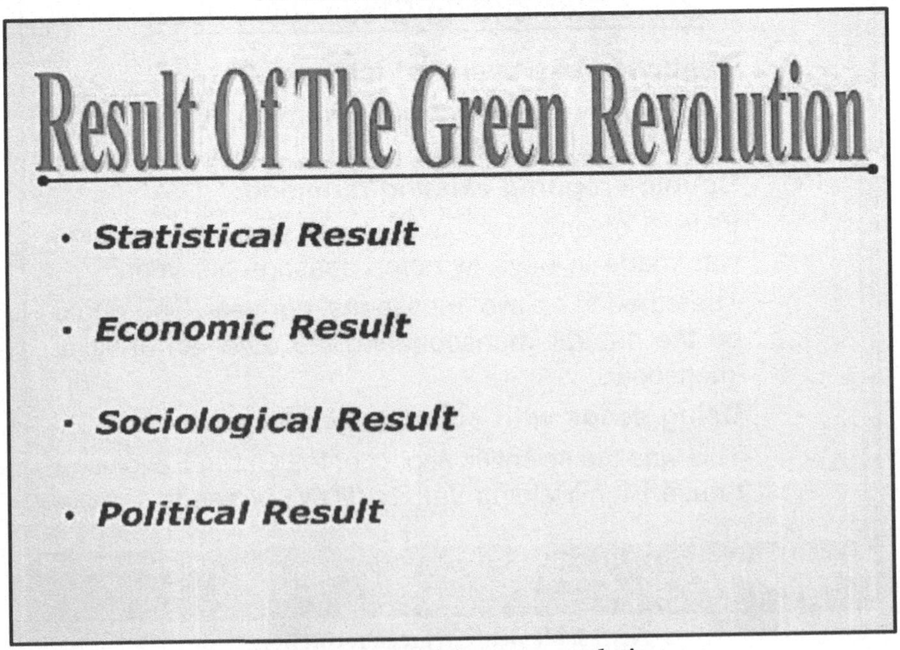

Fig. 9.8: Results of the green revolution
Source: based on review of literature

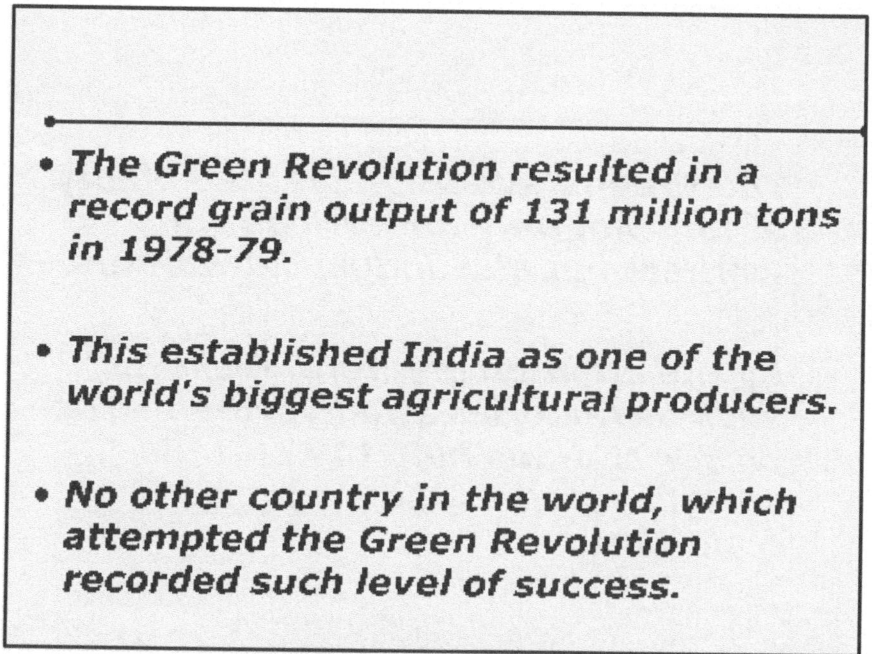

Fig. 9.9: Statically results
Source: based on review of literature

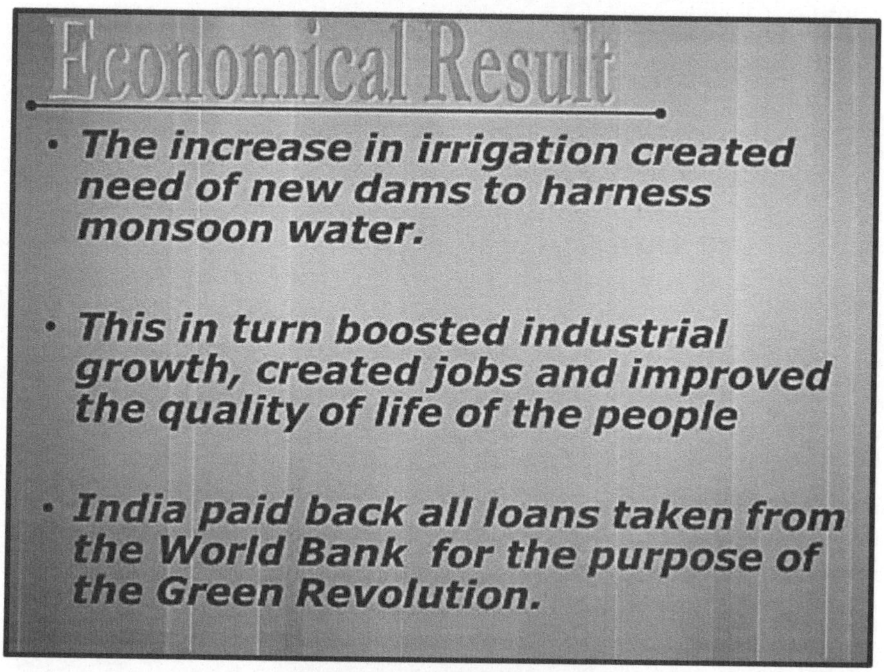

Fig. 9.10: Economical Results
Source: based on review of literature

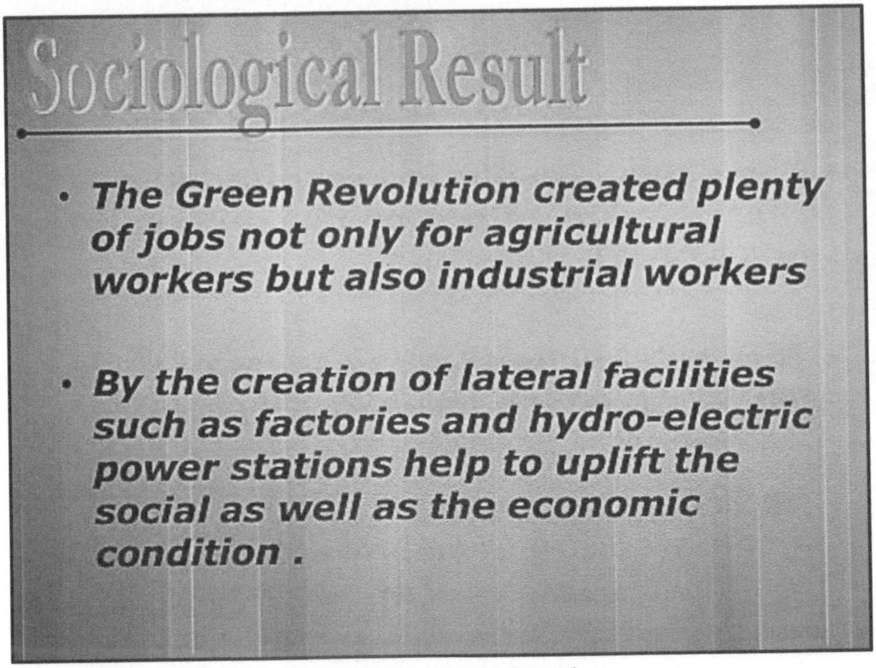

Fig. 9.11: Sociological result
Source: based on review of literature

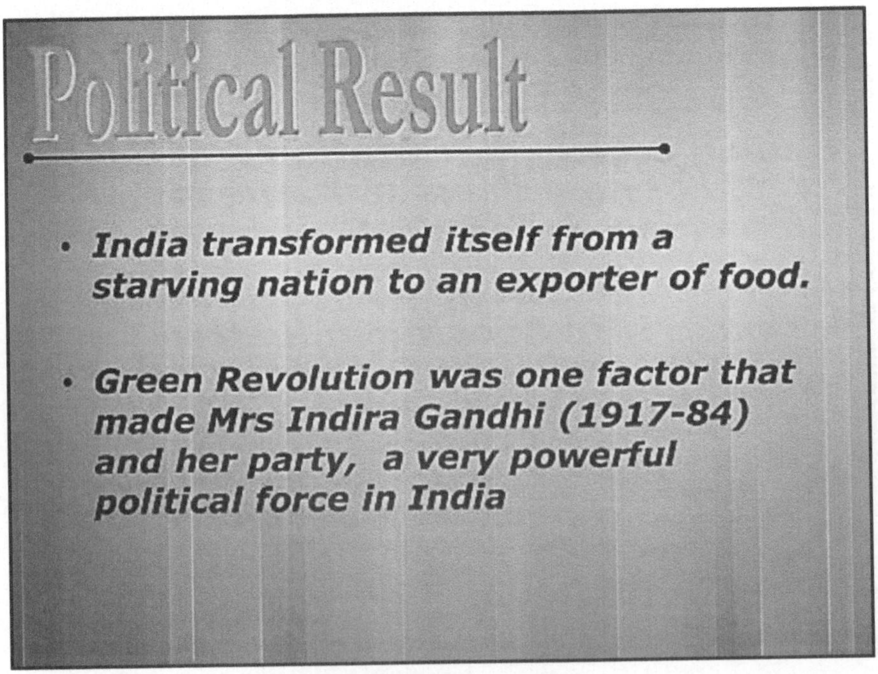

Fig. 9.12: Political result
Source: based on review of literature

Advantages of Green Revolution

1. Yields increased three times.
2. Multiple cropping.
3. Other crops grown which varied the diet.
4. Surplus to sell in cities creating a profit improving the standard of living.
5. Allows purchase of fertilizers, machienry etc.
6. India becomes self sufficient in food grains.

Fig. 9.13: Advantage of green revolution
Source: based on review of literature

Effects of Green Revolution

- ❑ Increase in Production
- ❑ Capitalistic Farming
- ❑ Effect on Rural Employment
- ❑ Reduction in Imports of food grains
- ❑ Development of Industries
- ❑ Effect on Prices
- ❑ Base for Economic Growth
- ❑ Effect on consumers
- ❑ Effect on Planning
- ❑ Increase in Trade
- ❑ Change in Thinking of Farmers

Fig. 9.14: Effect of Green revolution
Source: based on review of literature

Limitations of Green Revolution

1. The Green Revolution, however impressive, but NOT a 100% success.
2. Only Punjab and Haryana states showed best resuts of Green Revolution.
3. The new farming techniques, has given birth to the serious pollution of drinking water causing cancer and other diseases.
4. A recent **Punjabi University** study found a high rate of genetic damage among farmers, which was attributed to pesticide use.
5. The new organic fertilizer, pesticides and chemicals are ruining the soil.
6. Lead to unemployment and Rural-Urban Immigration.

Fig. 9.15: limitation of green revolution
Source: based on review of literature

Need for Second Green Revolution

- The time is now ripe for Second Green Revolution.
- India has tremendous export potential in agriculture in present era of globalization.
- In Second Green Revolution emphasis should be laid on:
  1. Non food grains
  2. Improving global market opportunities
  3. Improving rural infrastructure
  4. Improving irrigation, rural roads and rural electrification

Fig. 9.16: Need for second green revolution
Source: based on review of literature

CONCLUSION

The Green Revolution was a period when the productivity of global agriculture increased drastically as a result of new advances.Multiple cropping is when a field is used to grow two or more crops throughout the year, so that the field constantly has something growing on it. During this time period, new chemical fertilizers and synthetic herbicides and pesticides were created.High-yield crops are crops that are specifically designed to produce more overall yield. A method known as multiple cropping was also implemented during the Green Revolution and lead to higher productivity.These new farming techniques and advances in agricultural technology were utilized by farmers all over the world, and when combined, intensified the results of the Green Revolution.The chemical fertilizers made it possible to supply crops with extra nutrients and, therefore, increase yield. The newly developed synthetic herbicides and pesticides controlled weeds, deterred or kill insects, and prevented diseases, which also resulted in higher productivity.In addition to the chemical advances utilized during this time period, high-yield crops were also developed and introduced.

REFERENCES

https://en.wikipedia.org/wiki/Green_Revolution

edugreen.teri.res.in/explore/bio/green.htm

https://www.toppr.com/guides/economics/indian...1950.../green-revolution/

https://www.britannica.com/event/green-revolution

https://www.encyclopedia.com/plants-and-animals/.../green-revolution

https://www.merriam-webster.com/dictionary/green%20revolution

https://study.com/.../what-is-the-green-revolution-definition-benefits-and-is...

https://www.thehindubusinessline.com/...green-revolution/article27472671....

https://www.sciencedirect.com/topics/earth-and-planetary.../green-revolution

Pages: 134-146

Irrigation Practices and Sustainable Agriculture
Edited by: **Dr. Prasann Kumar and Dr. Pawan Kumar 'Bharti'**
ISBN: 978-93-88854-31-3
Edition: **2020**
Published by: **Discovery Publishing House Pvt. Ltd., New Delhi (India)**

10

Hydro Power for Sustainable Development of Society

Prasann Kumar[1,2*], Shipa Rani Dey[1]

GRAPHICAL ABSTRACT

Keywords: Agriculture, Biome, Cultivation, Water, Power

INTRODUCTION

Hydropower or water power (from Greek: □δωρ, "water") is power derived from the energy of falling water or fast running water,

[1] Department of Agronomy, School of Agriculture, Lovely Professional University, Jalandhar - 144 411 (Punjab) (India)
[2] Divison of Research and Development, Lovely Professional University, Jalandhar - 144 411 (Punjab) (India)

which may be harnessed for useful purposes. Since ancient times, hydropower from many kinds of watermills has been used as a renewable energy source for irrigation and the operation of various mechanical devices, such as gristmills, sawmills, textile mills, trip hammers, dock cranes, domestic lifts, and ore mills. A trompe, which produces compressed air from falling water, is sometimes used to power other machinery at a distance (https://en.wikipedia.org/wiki/Hydropowe).

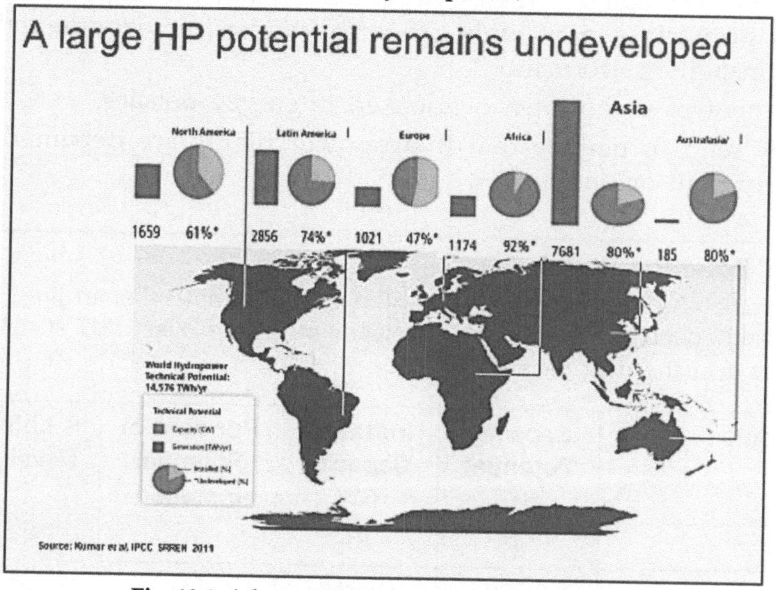

Fig. 10.1: A large HP potential remains undeveloped
Source: based on review of literature

GLOBAL POTENTIAL STATUS

The needs and the untapped potential are greatest in emerging and developing countries.

Hydropower development require over USD 40 billion per year over the next decades.

HYDROPOWER

- Hydropower is a proven renewable, mature, predictable, highest conversion efficiency and cost competitive energy source.
- Hydropower requires relatively high initial investment, but has the advantage of very low operation costs and a long lifespan, Part of multipurpose river valley projects, Quick start, stop and peaking.
- Life cycle analysis of hydropower shows as cleanest electricity technology with a low carbon footprint.
- Has the highest energy payback ratio.
- Solar & Wind energy need support from hydro.

- Being highest conversion efficiency and long time investment it yields benefits practically 5 to 10 times compared to other energy source like solar, wind.
- HP can support the penetration of other renewable by providing the backup that variable technologies need
- HP, regardless of size can be an opportunity for local, national and regional development when social and environmental impacts are dealt with properly – new tools exists to increase environmental and sustainability performance
- Hydropower is too often overlooked in energy policies.
- Many tend to believe that hydropower plants are detrimental to environment or unsafe.

Global Potential Status

The needs and the untapped potential are greatest in emerging and developing countries Hydropower development require over USD 40 billion per year over the next decades

Region	Capacity Potential GW	Installed Capacity GW	Per cent of Potential Installed	% Left to Develop
Africa	448	31	7	93
Asia	3,609	562	16	84
Australasia	61	14	23	77
Europe	412	182	44	56
North America	520	174	33	67
Latin Amarica	602	158	26	74
Total	**5,653**	**1,122**	**20**	**80**
India	**150**	**46**	**31**	**69**
Brazil	260	96	37	63
China	542	296	55	45

Source: Hydropower & Dams World Atlas, 2016

Fig. 10.2: Global potential status

Source: based on review of literature

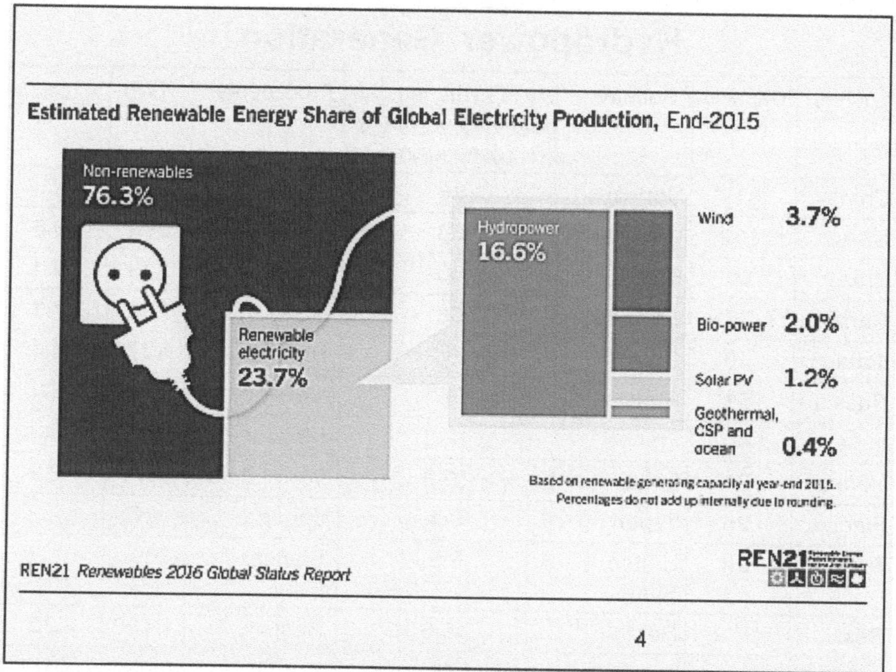

Fig. 10.3: Estimated Renewable Energy Share of Global Electricity Production
Source: based on review of literature

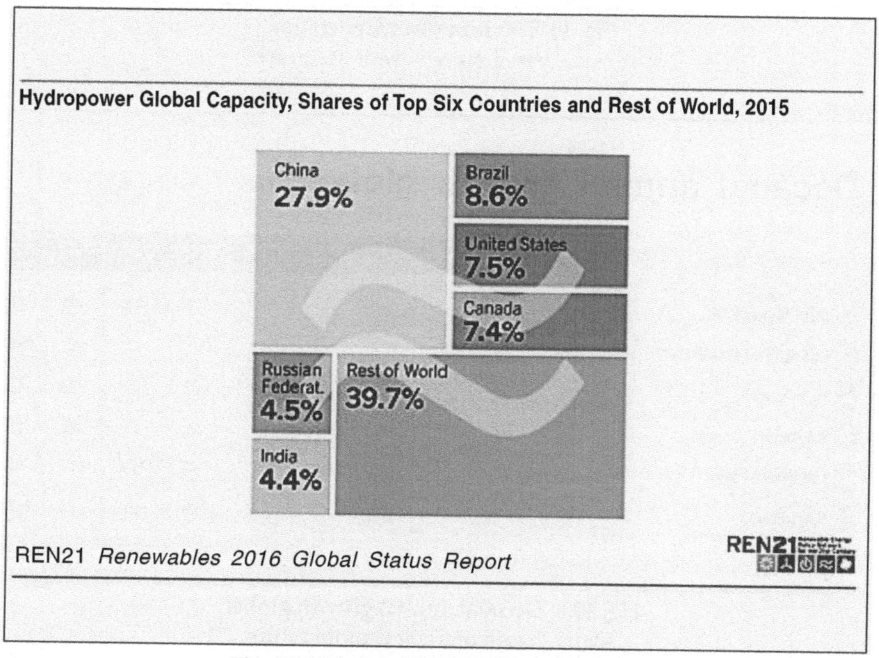

Fig. 10.4: Hydropower Global Capacity
Source: based on review of literature

Hydropower Generation

Country	Capacity (GW)	Country	% of hydro in total domestic electricity generation	Procedures	TWh	% of world total
China	311	Norway	96	China	1,064	26.7
USA	102	Venezuela	68	Canada	383	9.6
Brazil	89	Brazil	63	Brazil	373	9.4
Canada	76	Canada	58	USA	282	7.1
Japan	50	China	18.7	Russia	177	4.4
Russia	51	Russia	16.7	Norway	137	3.4
India	40	France	12.2	India	132	3.3
Norway	31	India	10.2	Venezuela	87	2.2
France	25	Japan	8.4	Japan	87	2.2
Turkey	24	United States	6.5	France	69	1.7
Rest	372	Rest	15.6	Rest	1,192	30
World	1,171	World	16.7	World	3,983	100

Source: Key World Energy STATISTICS, IEA, 2016

Fig. 10.5: Hydropower Generation
Source: based on review of literature

Decadal annual growth global

Total Installed Capacity		2004	2005	2006	2007	2008	2009	2010	2011	2012	2013
Solar Photovoltaic	GW	2.6	3.1	4.6	7.6	13.5	21	40	71	100	139
Concentrating Solar Power	GW	0.4	0.4	0.4	0.4	0.5	0.7	1.1	1.6	2.5	3.4
Wind Power	GW	48	59	74	94	121	159	198	238	283	318
Bio Power	GW	39	41	43	45	46	51	70	74	78	88
Geothermal Power	GW	8.9	9.8	10	10.4	10.7	11	11.2	11.4	11.7	12
Hydro Power	GW	715	–	–	920	960	980	935	960	990	1,000

Fig. 10.6: Decadal annual growth global
Source: based on review of literature

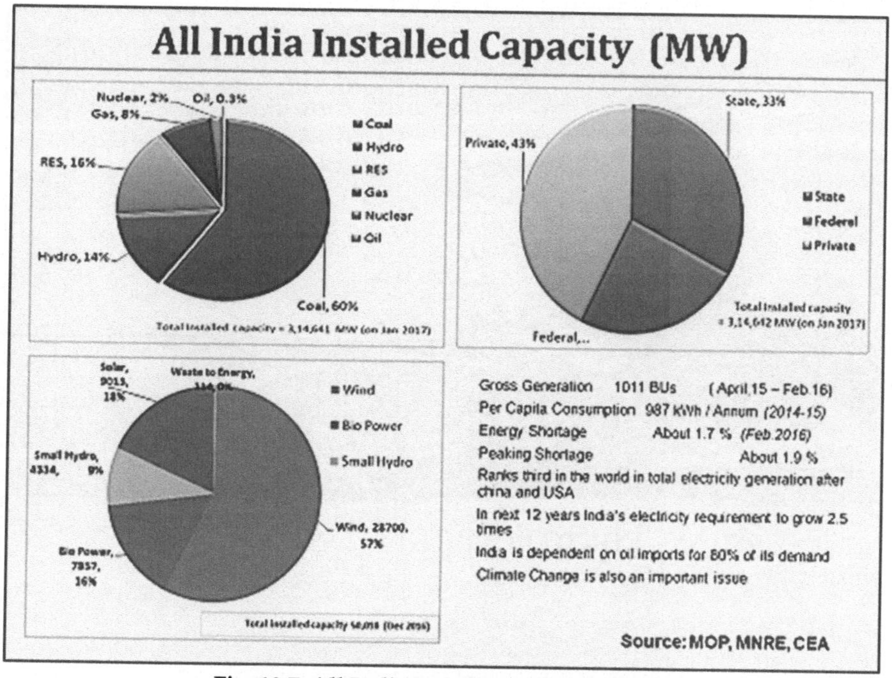

Fig. 10.7: All India Installed Capacity (MW)
Source: based on review of literature

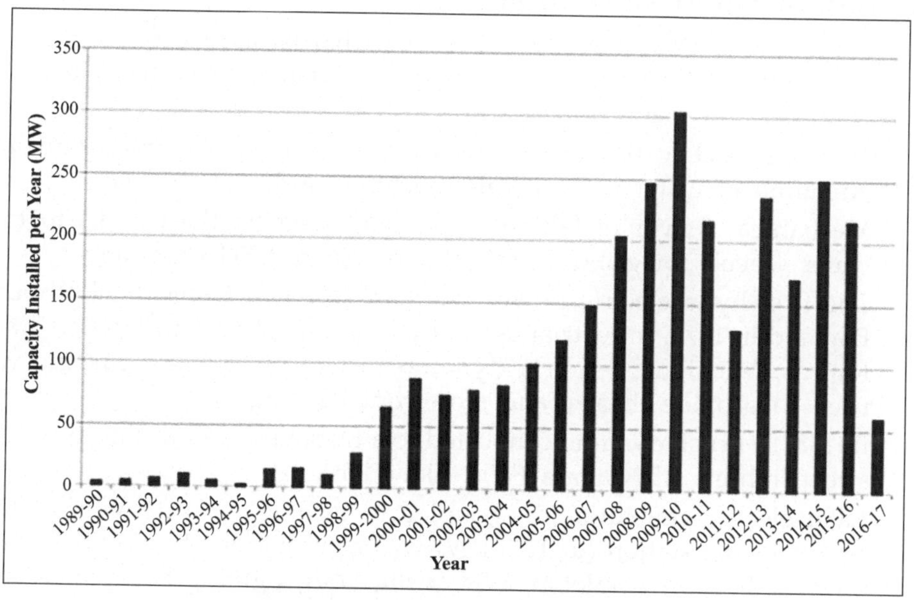

Fig. 10.8: Capacity installed per year
Source: based on review of literature

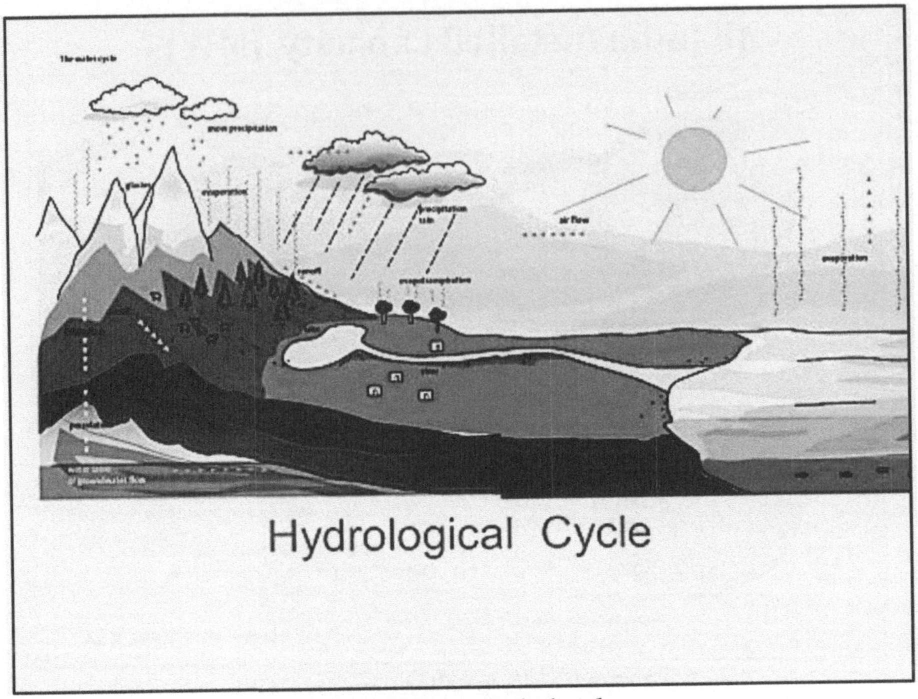

Fig. 10.9: Hydrological cycle

Source: based on review of literature

HISTORY OF SHP DEVELOPMENT

- Hydropower or water power is power that is derived from the force or energy of moving water from higher elevations to lower elevations harnessed for useful purposes.
- Prior to electric power, hydropower was used for irrigation and operation of water mills, textile machines and sawmills etc.
- Mechanical power of falling water was used by the Greeks to turn water wheels for grinding wheat more than 2,000 years ago.
- The first hydroelectric power plant installed in Cragside, Rothbury, England in 1870. Industrial use of hydropower started in 1880 in Grand Rapids, Michigan, when a dynamo driven by a water turbine was used to provide theatre and storefront lighting.
- In 1881, a brush dynamo connected to a turbine in a flour mill provided street lighting at Niagara Falls, New York.
- Later electric generator was coupled to turbine and thus world's first hydroelectric station (of 12.5 kW) was commissioned on 30 Sept 1882 on Fox River in Appleton, Wisconsin, USA, lighting two paper mills and a residence.

PURPOSE OF SHP

Social Sector SHPs:

- aims to supply electricity specially in stand alone mode
- characterized with poor load factor and of small capacity
- often involved in distribution also
- Often are fully supported by government
- O & M is recovered through user charges collection

Commercial SHPs:

- aims to sell electricity to power distributing or trading companies or for captive use
- are grid connected and are relatively larger capacity
- have high load factor
- Financially sound

Both are required and different level of approach, subsidy, tariff etc are needed

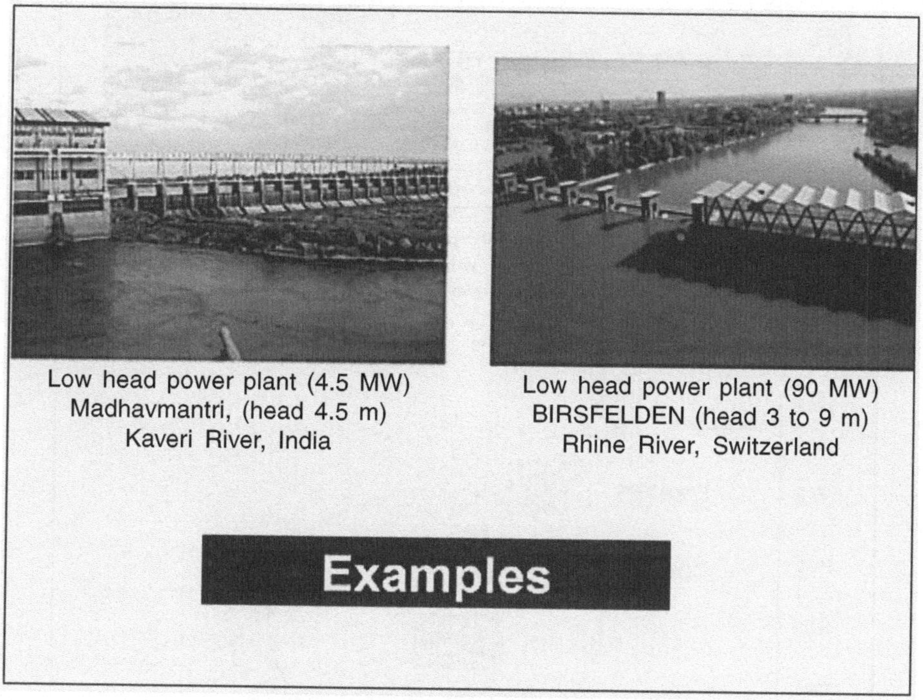

Fig. 10.10: Example of hydro power plant

Source: based on review of literature

TYPES OF SHP SCHEMES

- Run-of-river
- Canal fall based
- Dam Toe based
- In stream
- Pumped Storage

Fig. 10.11: Typesof hydropower
Source: based on review of literature

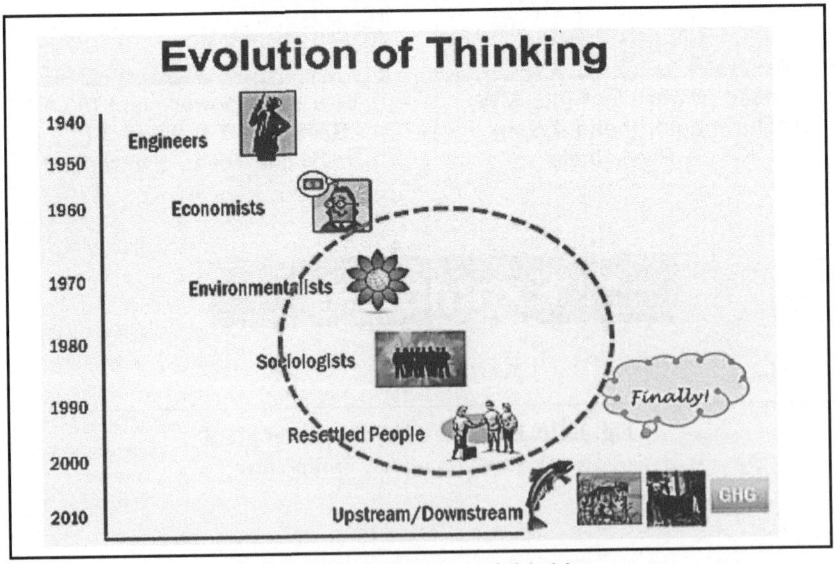

Fig. 10.12: Evaluation of thinking
Source: based on review of literature

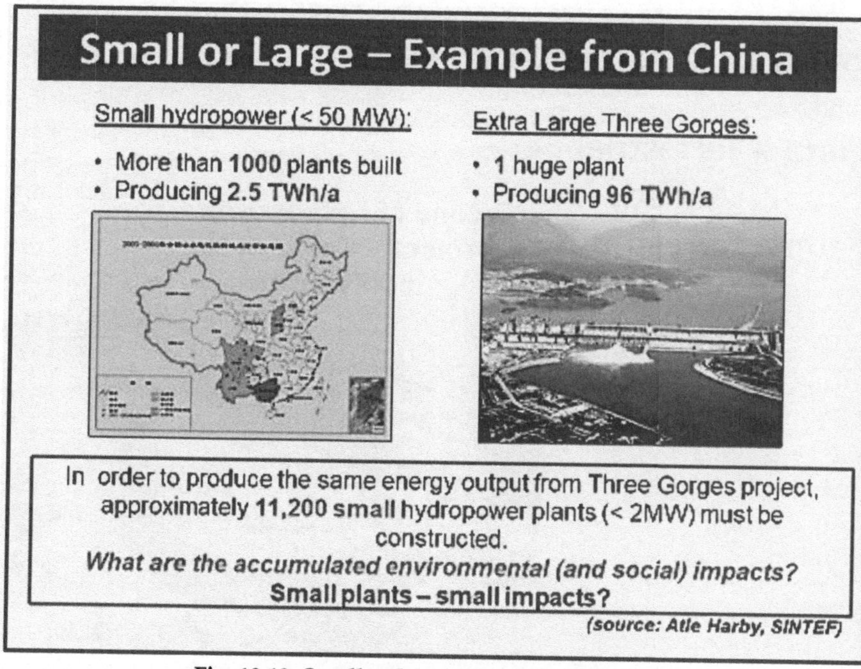

Fig. 10.13: Small or large- Example from china

Source: based on review of literature

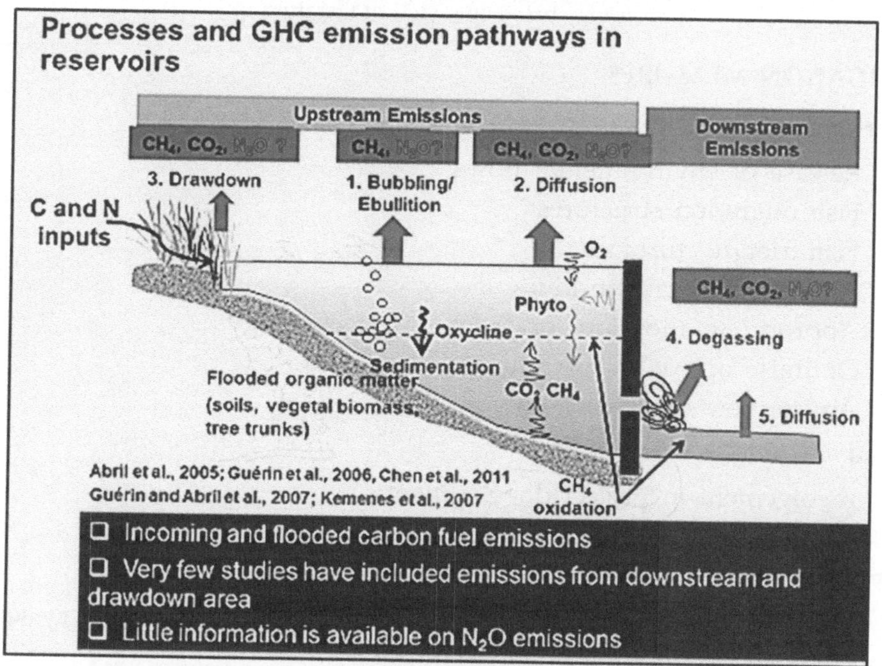

Fig. 10.14: Processes and GHG emission pathways in reservoirs

Source: based on review of literature

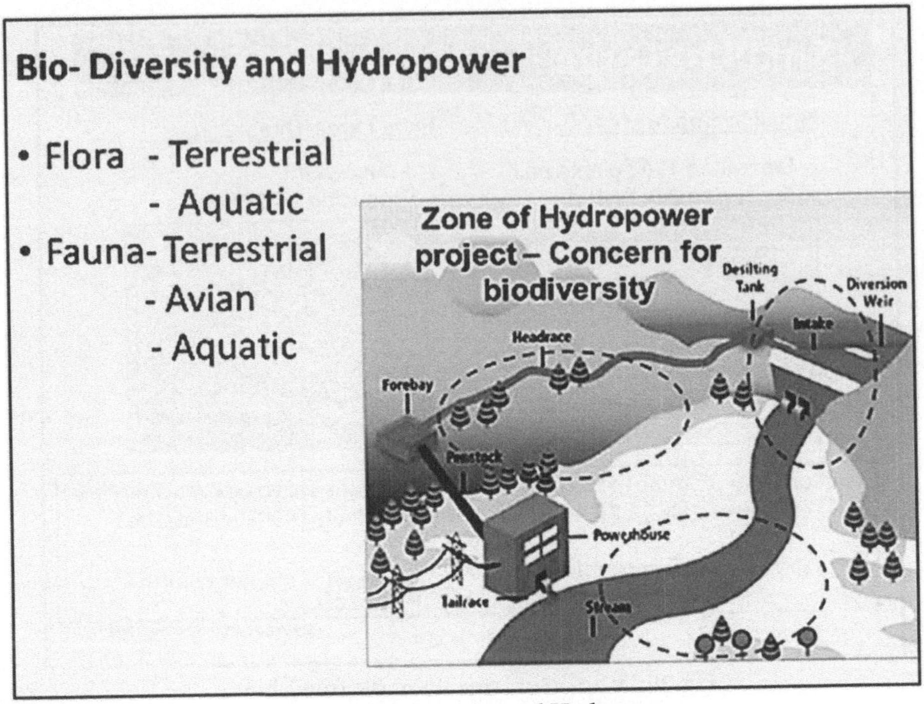

Fig. 10.15: Biodiversity and Hydropower
Source: based on review of literature

MITIGATION MEASURES

Environmental

- Release of environmental flows
- Fish migration structures
- Fish-friendly turbines
- Abrasive resistant turbines
- Appropriate adoption for Tunnelling technology
- Optimise operation for reducing flashiness
- Appropriate muck disposal

Social

- Involvement in project development
- Sharing the benefits of project

SHP AND ENVIRONMENT

To produce one kWh of electricity with the best renewable system – small hydro– has an environmental impact:

- 300 times lower than the one produced with lignite.

- 250 times lower in relation with the one generated with coal or petroleum.
- 125 times lower in relation with the one produced with uranium.
- 50 times lower than the one generated with natural gas

PROSPECTS FOR TECHNOLOGY IMPROVEMENT AND INNOVATION

- Variable speed technology
- Fish-friendly turbines
- Hydrokinetic turbines
- Abrasive resistant turbines
- Tunnelling technology
- Dam technology
- Optimization of operation
- Resource Assessment, Planning & Design
- Good controls

SHP AND ENVIRONMENT

To produce one kWh of electricity with the best renewable system – small hydro– has an environmental impact:

- 300 times lower than the one produced with lignite.
- 250 times lower in relation with the one generated with coal or petroleum.
- 125 times lower in relation with the one produced with uranium.
- 50 times lower than the one generated with natural gas.

BARRIERS TO SHP DEVELOPMENT

Technical Barriers

- Absence of feasibility reports Reports with Sufficient Details to take Investment Decisions
- Absence of basic data for the project like Hydrological data
- To increase plant load factor integration with other development and livelihood activities like irrigation, rural industries, education, health etc
- To connect to main electricity grid
- To have qualified and well trained personnel at all levels
- Absence of Manuals/Guidebooks/Hand books for various items of work

Institutional Barriers

- To provide basic data for the project
- Long time taken to collect hydrological data

- To provide conducive environment
- To provide guidance for development
- To provide attractive tariff by the users or utility

Financing Barriers

- To choose the optimum capacity of the plant
- To raise the long term finance
- To raise the contributions from the users
- To collect the user charges
- To meet the O & M expenditure
- To overcome the deficit in return on investment

Policy Barriers

- Undecided about the development priority of the area
- Hidden subsidies to other energy sources not taken into consideration
- Absence of integration of different sector development

Social Barrier

- Hesitation in participation in development process
- Lack of visualization for enhancing livelihood activities

CONCLUSION

Capacity development is the key to success for scaling up of SHP programme for planning, oversight, and monitoring; training to all project developers, facilitators, financial institutions and community members; adopting the standard equipment and designs

- Upfront public financing
- Encouraging higher participation of private sector
- Continued support R& D in several areas
- Clarity in Policies and regulations
- Setting up and enhancing institutions capacity

REFERENCES

https://en.wikipedia.org/wiki/Hydropower

https://www.eia.gov › Energy Explained › Renewable Sources

https://www.studentenergy.org/topics/hydro-power

https://www.renewableenergyworld.com/hydropower/tech.html

https://www.irena.org/hydropower

https://www.worldenergy.org/data/resources/resource/hydropower/

https://www.nationalgeographic.com/environment/global-warming/hydropower/

https://www.originenergy.com.au › Blog › About energy

https://www.hydropower.org/blog

Index

❑ ❑ ❑ ❑ ❑ ❑